ANCIENT GREEK & ROMAN RELIGION

Two Volumes in One

H. J. ROSE, M.A., F.B.A.

BARNES
&NOBLE
BOOKS
NEW YORK

Ancient Greek Religion originally published in 1946.
Ancient Roman Religion originally published in 1948.

This edition published by Barnes & Noble, Inc.

1995 Barnes & Noble Books

ISBN 1-56619-981-6

Printed and bound in the United States of America.
M 9 8 7 6 5 4 3 2 1

ANCIENT
ROMAN RELIGION

by

H. J. ROSE, M.A., F.B.A.

CONTENTS

PREFACE

In this little work, which is meant as a companion volume to that on the religion of ancient Greece, no more is attempted than to introduce the reader to some of the most outstanding features of the complicated religion, or rather series of religions, which flourished in Rome between the earliest recoverable ages of her long history and the close of the classical epoch. For brevity's sake, numerous statements have had to go without proof, and often something which is merely probable has been stated as if it were certain. It is hoped that readers unacquainted with the subject will not be seriously misled and that more than a few of them will be led on to read for themselves some at least of the longer, more elaborate and more technical works which are quoted in the bibliography at the end.

H. J. ROSE.

July 28th, 1948.

CHAPTER I

NVMEN

IN writing even a short account of the religion of ancient Rome an author is faced with a very different task from that which he must undertake if he would describe the pre-Christian cults of Greece.[1] In the latter case he must tell the story of a people who, at the earliest stage of which we have any documentary evidence, had gone a long way on the road which leads from a savage to a fully civilised conception of Deity and of man's place in the universe. The remnants of an earlier stage of thought have to be hunted for like fossils in the rocks and interpreted in the light of the manners and customs of populations that have remained very backward in their intellectual and spiritual development. The Greeks were keen, original thinkers, bold experimenters, capable of breaking with their past, if they thought it advisable, to a far greater degree than most nations. They had, moreover, a gift for abstract thought, and a remarkably high proportion of them had logical minds and were ready to follow their own ideas to the uttermost consequences. Hence they developed a highly abstract, largely monotheistic theology and read it into the traditional practices of their ancestral religion, and many of their conclusions, passing little changed into Christianity, have coloured the whole of European thought on such matters ever since. But the Romans were a much slower-witted people. Orderly and legalistic, willing to learn but at the same time extraordinarily tenacious of the past, at all events in form, they neither struck out any new lines for themselves nor ever quite abandoned the old, half-savage practices which they had inherited from simple ancestors, peasants and herdsmen of prehistoric days. Their theology and philosophy, when they had such things at all, were simplified adaptations of Greek

[1] These are briefly sketched in the author's *Ancient Greek Religion*, No. 5 of this series.

thought. Furthermore, the Greeks, the greatest artists of antiquity, had a vivid and pictorial imagination. The objects of their worship appeared to their mind's eye as clearly-defined figures, human in shape but glorious above the level of humanity, and as individual as any actual men or women. They had their peculiarities of dress and feature, their likes and dislikes, their loves and hates among themselves and towards men, and their relations of father and son, mother and daughter, sister and brother. The first attempts to systematise them were genealogies, and the beginning of history in Greece, so far as we know, was the setting down in verse, later in prose, of tales which chiefly concerned the gods and those mighty men, closely akin to the gods, who lived long ago, and were not an enfeebled race "such as mortals now are", to borrow Homer's recurrent phrase when he describes some prodigious feat of strength on the part of a Hektor or an Aias. But Rome had no mythology, or so little that it vanished before the brighter light of the Greek legends. The Greeks taught the Romans to write, in both senses of that phrase, for the Roman alphabet is derived from the Greek one, with few and trivial modifications, and all that the Romans ever knew of style was adapted from Greek models.

It follows that in dealing with Roman religion, the department in which that conservative people were most conservative, we can quite easily find, almost on the surface as it were, remnants of a very early and simple type of thought which, in Greece, we have to dig deep to recover. But, as Rome was never quite closed to foreign influences and at times received them eagerly, we have to add to these primitive remains a whole series of importations, adapted with the skill of born lawyers to the existing precedents and disguising their novelty under names and forms either of native origin or at least so modified as not to offend native feeling. These borrowings seem to have come, not so much from the nearest relatives of Rome, the other Italian peoples speaking languages akin to Latin and having apparently much the same historical origins as the dwellers by the Tiber, as from foreigners, first the Etruscans, then the Greeks (if indeed some of the earliest borrowings were not from Greek communities in Italy), then from Orientals, till at last the greatest of the eastern religions, Christianity, overcame all the rest, and, moulded by Roman organisers and systematisers, assumed its Western form, profoundly influenced by the Eastern Churches yet readily distinguishable from them.

In one respect the getting of facts about early and classical Roman cult is easier than the gathering of them for Greece. We are dealing with the religious history of one community, not of a multiplicity. We know, it is true, a fair amount concerning the rites and customs of other Italian cities in ancient times, but nothing like enough to write a complete account of any one of them. We may, therefore, for the purposes of the present short study, confine ourself to Roman evidence, perhaps taking an illustrative parallel now and then from some other place. In another way, the task is harder than for Greece. The Greeks were always a vocal people, not only interested in their own customs and thoughts, but given to speaking and, what is more to the point for a historian, writing about them at considerable length. Hence we have documents in fair abundance, though vastly more have been lost, for nearly all periods from early in the first millennium B.C. down to the end of antiquity. But early Rome wrote next to nothing, compared to early Greece, and what little there was not only is lost to us but had mostly perished when the authors who have come down to us were born. Cicero and Varro, Vergil and Livy, to say nothing of many others, were much interested from various points of view in the religion of their country ; but not only were they hampered by imperfect documents concerning at least the origins and early history of that subject, but what material they had they perforce interpreted in the light of what they had themselves been taught, the Greek methods of writing history and the Greek schools of philosophy. Most of the conclusions reached by the latter were quite false for native Roman beliefs, and the methods of the former, by no means perfectly adapted to the study of Greece herself, were still less so for dealing with Rome, or with Italy generally. Thus we find that the first care of a Roman political historian is to produce a tale of the origins of his native country modelled on Greek foundation-legends and crammed with fancies quite foreign to Italy ; while so able a man as Varro, for instance, when he tries to give an intelligible account of what his ancestors believed, is hampered at every turn by his own desire to find, what was never there, the expression of ideas which certain Greek thinkers conceived as fundamental to any religious system, these in their turn being handicapped by lack of knowledge of the way simple minds really work when they try to achieve right relations with the unknown powers, actual or imagined, on which their lives and prosperity depend, or are thought by them to depend. However, we can gather from such materials as are at our disposal many useful facts and interpret them in the light of our own broader knowledge, the harvest of investigations into the lives and thoughts of the more backward of mankind which have now been going on scientifically and with increasingly good method for some generations.

I said in discussing Greek religion that two ideas, whether or not they can be claimed as the first beginnings of religious beliefs and consequent practices, are certainly early and will serve to start from in dealing with the cults of a people who had risen above savagery when first we hear of them. One of these is animism, the conception of all manner of objects in the visible world as having in them something like the soul which, crudely enough pictured in most cases, is postulated as governing the bodies of men and beasts. The other is what has been called dynamism, the notion that there exists a kind of power, different from that power which is to be observed in ordinary muscular exertions and so forth, in which numerous favoured men and, still more, sundry non-human beings, varying from beasts to ghosts and gods, and also various processes, generally of a magical kind, are thought to share. This is most commonly called, in this country, by its Polynesian and Melanesian name of *mana*, which seems originally to signify no more than "force," or, for it can be an adjective as well as a substantive, "forceful, potent". The classical description of it was given in 1891 by Bishop Codrington in his fundamental work *The Melanesians*, the product of his own long residence among that people and his accurate study of their mental processes ; for, being a missionary of the best and most intelligent type, he conceived rightly that it was his duty to know the men and women whom he tried to bring to his own religious opinions. His account of *mana* is given on p. 118 of his book.

"The Melanesian mind", he says, "is entirely possessed by the belief in a supernatural power or influence, called almost universally *mana*. This is what works to effect everything which is beyond the ordinary power of men, outside the common processes of nature ; it is present in the atmosphere of life, attaches itself to persons and things, and is manifested by results which can only be ascribed to its operation. . . . But this power, though itself impersonal, is always connected with some person who directs it ; all spirits have it, ghosts generally, some men." A little later he adds : "The Melanesians believe in the existence of beings personal, intelligent, full of *mana*, with a certain bodily form which is visible but not fleshly like the bodies of men. These they think to be more or less actively concerned in the affairs of men, and they invoke and otherwise approach them." He goes on to explain that some of these beings are ghosts, others what he, perhaps a little rashly, styles "spirits".

A great deal of what the good Bishop says of his Melanesian parishioners could be taken over with little change when we speak of the earliest Roman ideas of which we can form any adequate conception. The Romans, like the Melanesians (and Polynesians) of modern times, believed in "a supernatural power or influence", which they called *numen*, plural *numina*. This word, which seems literally to signify a movement, perhaps especially a nod of the head (the verb *nuere*, with which it is connected, means to nod) would appear to have developed the sense of "result of action, sign of a force or power at work". Until the time of Augustus it never is used to mean any personal or individual god, and even then it is not often so misunderstood by good writers such as Vergil or Ovid. But it is something which gods possess. Juppiter the sky- and weather-god, in Horace, makes a crust of ice form over the snow *puro numine*, by his unmixed or unimpeded *numen*. In plain prose, it is a clear, frosty night.

Speaking of the great corn-goddess of Henna in Sicily, whom he calls Ceres but the Sicilian Greeks Demeter, Cicero informs his audience that abundant miracles make plain her power (*uis*, the ordinary word for force) and—here he adds the exactly right word—her *numen*. Verres, the scoundrely governor of Sicily whom he is impeaching, had possessed *uis*, as any man might, but the worst of his offence had been that he had set at naught the *numen* of the goddess and stolen one of the holiest adornments of her ancient shrine. Varro, explaining *numen* by the famous Homeric passage in which Zeus, by a mere nod of assent, makes the holy mountain Olympos shake, says it belongs to him whose authority is greatest, in other words to a supernatural being ; and Cicero again, speaking of the Stoic Supreme Being, says that all things obey his *numen*. But *numen* is not confined to gods. A single man does not seem to have it until we come to Imperial times, when it was the proper and loyal thing to say, or at least imply, that an Emperor was something more than mortal, and we hear quite often of the *numen* of the reigning one. But even under the Republic, a body of men sometimes possess it, for the Roman Senate, the most powerful assembly of human beings that existed anywhere in the civilised world for several generations, is said occasionally to have it ; it is true that the speaker is always using highly complimentary language when he talks in this strain, but clearly it is not felt that the compliment is out of all proportion to the facts and exceeds the limits of tasteful flattery. By the exercise of their authority, the senators collectively, though not individually, can do things "beyond the ordinary power of men". So can the sovran people of Rome, when they exercise the powers which are lawfully theirs, and therefore Cicero, addressing them in laudatory terms after they had decreed his recall from exile, tells them that he will reverence their *numen* no less than that of the gods themselves. A god can confer *numen* on a mortal. When one of the Imperial house was starting for the East, to secure what could be construed as at all events a diplomatic victory against Rome's one serious opponent, the Parthian Empire, Ovid, always decorously loyal, was ready with a prayer that Mars the war-god and Caesar (Augustus, the reigning emperor) would give him *numen* on his journey. Even inanimate things, if there is something holy or uncanny about them, may have, or even be *numen*. Hesiod, says Manilius the astrologer-poet, sang of "the gods of the woodland and the *numina* sacred to the Nymphs". I fail to see what he can mean save that the wild places which the Nymphs and their Italian equivalents were thought to frequent were themselves examples of a mysterious and superhuman activity, that the streams, caves, old forest trees and other such objects, which owed nothing to the hand of man and stood outside his fields and dwellings, were as weird and fairy-like as the divine or semi-divine creatures which the country folk of Manilius' day still supposed to haunt them. More commonly, it would be said or felt that there was *numen* in such places ; Ovid again tells us that there was in old days a grove of holm-oaks on the Aventine Hill at Rome, "at sight whereof you might say, 'There is *numen* here' ". A natural conclusion, but not inevitable, would be that some deity lived in the grove and the *numen* belonged to him. So in Vergil, Euander, the legendary leader of a band of Arkadian settlers supposed to have created the first settlement on the site of the future Rome, tells Aeneas, as he shows him the Capitoline Hill, where in later days the great temple of Juppiter, Juno and Minerva was to stand, that :

"what god it is we know not, but some god lives in this grove and on this tree-clad hilltop. My Arkadians believe that they have often seen Juppiter himself there" (being a Greek, he would of course call him Zeus) "shaking his dark mantle of goat-skin in his right hand as he marshalled his storm-clouds".

But more than this ; men themselves could on occasion confer *numen*, or at least persuade it to come where it was wanted, by performing the proper rites. A boundary-mark (*terminus*) was no trifling matter to Roman farmers, whose whole wealth consisted in the produce of their land and of such cattle, large and small, as they might possess. It was important to know exactly where Gaius' land ended and Seius' field began, and the Hebrew curse on him who removeth his neighbour's landmark would have been heartily echoed by any Italian of early days. Indeed something very like it occurred in their own formulae. There was an old law, so old that its origin was quite unknown, and therefore it was ascribed to Numa Pompilius, the second of the traditional line of kings, of whom we can say only that he bore a good Italian name and so may have been a real person before he was buried under a heap of edifying stories of Greek origin, such as any who will may read at large in Plutarch's *Life* of him. But whoever enacted it, this old statute laid down that if any man ploughed up a boundary-mark, both he and the oxen who drew his plough should be *sacri*, outlawed, a word we shall have to deal with later on, but for the present it is enough to remark that if a man was *sacer* he had no human rights whatever, and anyone who chose to kill him might do so with impunity. Later times had grisly tales to tell of the divine vengeance which would fall on the wrong-doer, ending in the complete destruction of him and all his house. Therefore, to set up a *terminus* was a business to be conducted decently and in order, with due observance of ritual, and we are so fortunate as to know how the Romans went about it.

Siculus Flaccus, a late but well-informed author on land-surveying, after mentioning with regret the abandonment of ancient custom, tells us how a boundary-mark was set in the old days. "They used to stand the stones themselves on the surface of the ground near the places where they meant to dig holes and fix them. The stones they would anoint, veil and garland. In the holes made for the stones to go into, when they had made sacrifice and burned the flesh of the slain victim on blazing sticks, they would, with their heads veiled, let some of the blood drip, and also throw in incense and grain. They would add honey-combs, wine and other materials customary for the ritual of boundary-stones. When all the offering was burned, they would set the stones on top of the hot ashes and then fix them carefully".

Now if, as our author assures us, the stones themselves were treated in this respectful fashion, and afterwards set into holes prepared by being used as the place of a sacrifice, the holy remnants of which were still there when the stone was lowered into place and fixed, clearly the boundary-mark was in close contact with things remote from the everyday world, the condition of non-holiness which the South Seas call *noa*, and thus transferred into the condition which that region of the globe knows as *tapu* or *tabu*, Latin as *sacer*. We are thus better enabled to understand Ovid when he says, addressing the boundary stone, or the god Terminus, for the two are one, "whether you are a stone or a stake fixed in the ground, you too have *numen*". Care had indeed been taken to give it a sufficiency of that desirable quality, by the farmers whose lands the mark bounded, as Siculus Flaccus explains later. Nor were they content with doing all this once, for every year the proprietors between whose lands the holy objects lay used to meet at or near them and offer sacrifice again. When such precautions were duly observed, neighbours might hope that no quarrels would arise between them, and presumably that the mere ordinary and unconsecrated sticks or stones which were put where necessary to mark out the rest of the boundary line would be kept in order and at their posts of duty by their "numinous" fellows. It is to be noticed that not a word of the descriptions that have come down to us suggests that a spirit or god was conjured into the stone ; it has *mana*, *numen*, and that is all. A Terminus was indeed worshipped on the Capitol, whether because it marked out some ancient precinct there or as a sort of representative of all boundary-marks in Roman territory, but Ovid's remark applies to any and every object of this kind which had been put into the ground with proper ceremony.

I have said that the sacrifice was annual, besides the original rite which made the stone once and for all holy. Sacrifice, to a Roman, was indeed an act of piety, but not gratuitous, for the sacrificer expected something in return, nor purely and simply a conventional way of showing what he would call *pietas*, dutiful affection, towards a celestial benefactor. There is very good evidence that the recipient, even if he was one of the greatest gods, was thought to be the better for it. While it was being performed, as the gift, regularly including food of some kind, was laid on the altar or otherwise conveyed to the recipient, the sacrificer would commonly say, "Be thou *macte* by this offering". *Macte* is an old word, apparently to begin with the vocative of a participle which signified "increased". It is hard to imagine in what the god was supposed to be "increasèd" if it was not in his store of *mana*. He had, no doubt, much *numen* of his own, but his activities would surely result in drawing on his capital of power. What if he spent it and had none left for the further benefits which would be needed by his worshippers ? Prudence, and the Romans were a very prudent people, not least so in business matters, suggested that if there was to be so much expenditure, there ought also to be a steady income, and, it would seem, this was supposed to be furnished by the sacrifices. Just how this was imagined to happen is not always clear ; we have neither complete accounts of all rituals in use among the ancients nor any authoritative exposition of the older ideas underlying or deduced from the ritual actions. But here and there a valuable piece of information enables us to make a good guess. One of the best examples is the festival known as the Fordicidia. The name means "the killing of the *forda*", and *forda* is a cow in calf. On April 15th of every year such a cow was slaughtered by each of the *curiae*, the very old divisions into which the citizen body originally fell, and another on the Capitol by the pontiffs, of whom we shall have more to say in another chapter. Parallels to such a sacrifice are to be found, for instance, in Greece, and the underlying idea is pretty plain. April is a warmer month in Italy than here, and much nearer harvest time. Earth is then manifestly busy preparing the crops which are growing on her surface, and Earth, Tellus Mater, is the goddess to whom the sacrifice is made. She is using a vast deal of *numen* in bestowing on the people who plough and sow her fields (for Tellus is no personification of the planet on which we live, but much more nearly the owner of the *numen* or *mana* of those portions of the surface which Latin-speaking farmers cultivated) the foodstuffs which they want, and it is well to renew her supplies, lest she become unfertile. Now the cows have shown that they possess fertility, in other words a certain amount of *numen*, for obviously *numen* is needed to produce offspring, else why are some women and some beasts barren, though they appear perfectly healthy ? Normally, they would use their *numen* in bringing forth living calves ; divert it, then, to the more immediately pressing needs of Tellus, and her lowered balance at the magical bank on which the gods draw is satisfactorily increased. All this does not mean that the Romans of any age which has left us a particle of evidence were too ignorant of agriculture to put barnyard manure on their fields or otherwise restore to the soil something at least of the chemical constituents it had lost in producing grain. Far from it ; we even hear of a godling called Sterculinus (*stercus* is the regular word for dung) who superintended the business of manuring, and much that their writers tell us indicates that they went about their task of raising cereals in a thoroughly business-like and practical manner. But to their ideas, which were substantially those of all farmers until quite late times, part of practical agriculture was the processes necessary to keep up the supply of *mana* which is needed if the ground is to perform its recurrent miracle of giving men many grains of corn for every one they have given it. Mysterious though *numen* may be, and much though its proper handling may need the guidance of experts, its use is a matter of every day, not of occasional festivals and high days.

Since, however, so much care was taken to keep the Roman earth well supplied with *mana*, or *numen*, there are signs that its power could be used for other purposes than growing corn. When early Rome had to deal with foreign nations (and foreigners' magic is dangerous the world over), it was done through certain officials called *fetiales*. These were formally directed by the king what they were to do, and one of them then asked the king for *sagmina*. The answer was, "Take them clean" (*pura tollito*) and the *fetialis* tore up some grass, with the earth sticking to its roots, from the holy ground of the Roman citadel. With this he proceeded to touch the head and hair of one of his colleagues, thus making him the chief and active member of the deputation, who would actually recite the terms of the treaty it was proposed to make and perform the necessary ritual to make them binding. Obviously, it is no light matter to engage the honour of one's state in this way, and is not made lighter by the ancient conception of it, not as primarily a matter of honour or international morality, but as a process which would bring down the immediate vengeance of the sky-god on Rome if the terms were not kept. Therefore the person entrusted with this delicate task needs all the *numen* he can get, and it would appear that some of the *numen* of his native soil was transferred to him for the occasion. The immediate source of it is the goddess Tellus, or perhaps the presiding deity of the citadel, Juno ; but human hands have performed the actual transfer. Man cannot, it would seem, originate *numen*, but he is capable of directing it, in this as in many other rites.

Mana in the Pacific region, *numen* in Rome, can attach itself to certain inanimate things ; Earth is not one of these, for she was not considered inanimate. To return for a moment to Bishop Codrington, he states that *mana* may be conveyed in such things as a stone amulet, a tuft of leaves or a tooth, all of which may be useful war-charms if properly used. A prosperous Melanesian cultivator owes his good fortune to "stones full of *mana* for pigs and yams". Hence it need not surprise us that in Rome there are distinct signs of *numen* about so holy a thing as an altar. It can be "increased" by putting some offering, even a trifling one, upon it ; but apart from such contact as this, it is too holy, or too dangerous, a thing to touch.   There is a well-known passage in Horace, a humorously kindly address to a simple and pious country-woman, in which he assures her that if she is guilty of such a sin (he implies that it is the only one at all likely in her case, and no doubt, since a domestic altar is meant, it is one which might occur while she was tidying her house) the simplest of offerings, a handful of salted grain, would be enough to recover the favour of the little household gods she has offended. In more serious cases, it was usual to touch an altar when taking an oath ; for an oath contains a conditional curse by the swearer, who calls for divine vengeance on himself if he is perjured. He is thus deliberately coming into contact with the power which will smite him if he deserves it.

However, an altar is regularly the altar of some deity, although instances occur in which the name of the god is unknown and the holy object dedicated "to whoever it is, god or goddess" (*si deus si dea*). There are material objects so very full of *numen* as actually to bear specific divine names. For example, in the Regia, the ancient palace of Roman kings, or the later constructions which occupied its site and bore its name, there were certain holy spears, with which war-magic was performed on occasion. This in itself is not very remarkable, but it sounds somewhat strange to modern notions that the spears themselves seem to have borne the name of the god Mars. It puzzled the later Romans, some of whom modified the name by speaking of the "spears *of* Mars" instead, but there is no real reason to doubt that to begin with Mars and the spears were one and the same. We know, from a bit of antiquarian learning preserved in the commentary on Vergil bearing the name of Servius, that when war was about to begin the Roman commander "went into Mars' shrine and first moved the sacred shields, next the spear carried by the image itself, saying, 'Mars, awake' ". But we also know that in old days there was no image of Mars or anyone else to hold a spear in its hand ; the earliest war-leaders, therefore, shook the *numen*-charged arms themselves, and in so doing aroused the *mana* of their god. The sanctuary no doubt was in the Regia, and the interesting and significant thing is that the arms *were* Mars. In like manner there is good proof, though details of the matter are not free from doubt, that a stone or stones, probably the latter, preserved on the Capitol, were Juppiter, distinguished from other manifestations of the great sky-god by their name, Juppiter the Stone (*Iuppiter Lapis*).

This brings us to a consideration of what a Roman of early days supposed a god to be. Since *numen* is found in sundry places and attached to various persons and things, it is not remarkable that its manifestations were sometimes less and sometimes more potent. If they were strong, and especially if they were regular in their occurrence, the natural conclusion would be that they were produced by a kind of person who had much *numen* and was ready to display it for the benefit of those who approached him in the proper manner. This person was a god or goddess, and concerning the nature of these beings the Roman, left to his own devices, seems to have had a great incuriosity. A god exercised his *numen* at certain times and places or under certain circumstances. Something generally, not always, indicated whether the power behind the action was male or female, a *deus* or a *dea*. Honorific titles were often bestowed on these powers, among the commonest being "father" and "mother", words, it is to be noted, which have no etymological connexion with begetting or bearing, whether applied to deities or to human beings. This point was made long ago by Fustel de Coulanges in his famous work *La cité antique ;* his words are still well worth quoting.

"The very name by which he (the head of a Roman household) is called, *pater*, contains some curious information. The word is the same in Greek, Latin and Sanskrit. . . . What did it mean and what idea did it evoke then in men's minds ? We can know, for it kept that meaning in formulae belonging to religious and legal language. When the ancients invoked Juppiter under the title of *pater* of gods and men, they did not mean that he was their [physical] father, for they never supposed he was, but on the contrary believed that the human race had existed before he did. The same title was given to Neptune, Apollo, Bacchus, Vulcan and Pluto, whom men certainly did not suppose to be their fathers, while the title of *mater* was applied to Minerva, Diana and Vesta, all three of whom were supposed to be virgin goddesses. Similarly, in legal language, the title of *paterfamilias* [literally, father of the household] could be given to a man who had no children, was not married, was not even old enough to enter upon a marriage".

Some of the examples from religious formulae confuse pure Latin with Latinised Greek usages, but the general conclusion is not to be upset ; *pater*, the Latin word cognate to "father" and closest akin to it in meaning, signifies not so much him who has begotten a younger person as him who has natural authority over one inferior in age or status, and, with a difference of sex, the same is true of *mater*, or mother. Therefore, when we find these titles applied to Roman gods, we need not ask what other beings, divine or human, were supposed to be their children, for the words do not imply any such relationship. One of the many indications of this is that in all native Italian cult there is but one doubtful instance of the natural correlative, to our notions, of the words "father" and "mother". Two inscriptions, of Praeneste, the modern Palestrina, not of Rome, call Fortuna the daughter of Juppiter. We have our choice between misunderstanding of a formulae still older than these ancient records and a rather early intrusion of Greek mythology, or personification, in which Tyche, or Chance, is sometimes the daughter of Zeus.

If the Romans therefore were so incurious about the persons of their deities as not even to try to arrange them in genealogies, it is not to be expected that they would invent many stories about their doings, other than their wonderful works towards men. Of these, indeed, there are a few. For instance, miracles of Vesta, the hearth-goddess, of whom more will be said later, seem now and then to have been told. It was said that once her holy fire went out, and Aemilia, one of the Vestal Virgins, was responsible, for she had left the tending of it to a novice. This was bad enough, but it began to be rumoured that some impious deed had profaned the holy place. Aemilia therefore prayed that, if she had served Vesta faithfully and in purity of body and mind, the goddess would manifest herself and save her priestess. With that she tore a strip from her dress and threw it upon the cold ashes, whereupon a great flame sprang up in testimony of the divine approval. Another Vestal, Tucca by name, was accused of the worst of offences for one in her office, unchastity. Called upon to defend herself, she replied that she would do so in deeds, not in words, and invoking Vesta, proceeded to the Tiber, where she drew water in a sieve, carried it to the Forum, and poured it out before the feet of the pontiffs assembled to try her. Another tale and a famous one concerned no well-known divinity but one whose very name was hidden from his worshippers. Before the Gaulish invasion of 390 B.C., a certain Marcus Caedicius was out of doors late one night when a voice, louder and clearer than any man's, bade him warn the magistrates that the Gauls were coming. He reported this prodigy, but no one paid any attention to it, and the Gauls, routing a Roman army, took the city and held it to ransom. When they were gone, it was felt that some measures should be taken to express a proper feeling towards the power which had done its best to make known the danger to them, but, no one having any idea what being had pronounced the mysterious words, a chapel was erected in honour of the Speaker who gave utterance (Aius Locutius). Certainly there had been *numen* at work, but where a Greek would have set about finding, to his own satisfaction at least, what god it was, and probably would have added a suitable title to the name of some existing deity, the Romans were content to describe him in terms of the one fact relating to him which they knew. Whether the story is true or false, the chapel was real, and was still there in Livy's days, for he gives its position (it was near Vesta's shrine, on the thoroughfare called New Street), as well as telling the legend.

It hardly needs to be pointed out how sharp a contrast all this makes to the rich mythology of Greece, to say nothing of other peoples, such as the Aryan Indians. Hardly a Greek god, however minor, was without his legends, telling of his birth, his relation to other deities, his loves and quarrels, and all that is necessary to make a clearly defined personality. Even so pale a figure as Hestia, the equivalent of Vesta in Greek cult, was humanised in this way, for at least it was known whose daughter she was ; her parents were Kronos and Rhea, and she remained virgin at her own request, having no taste for marriage, though more than one god proposed for her. Vesta, despite her miracles, can hardly be called a person, and Ovid was reflecting not only the facts of cult but the usual conception of the goddess when he bade his readers understand that she was "nothing other than living flame".

Indeed, some features of early Roman cult reveal not so much a polytheism as a polydaimonism, the worship, that is, of an indefinite number of quite small figures, defined as regards their functions but in other respects mere names. This tendency was greatly elaborated by the official regulation of the cult, for nothing was more eagerly sought than to address precisely the right power at the right time. In the official records of names, titles and functions of the deities, known as *indigitamenta*, there were contained long lists of gods and goddesses whose *numen* manifested itself in highly specialised ways. For instance, there were associated with Ceres the corn-goddess and Tellus, of whom we have already spoken, no fewer than twelve minor figures, every one of whom has a name significant of some part of the cycle of farm-work. They begin with Vervactor, whose *numen* extends no further than to enable the cultivator to plough fallow land (*ueruagere*), and they end with Promitor, whose function is simply the taking out of the corn from its store-place to make flour, or perhaps to sow. Highly artificial though these lists are, they rest upon a real tendency of the Romans, to recognise with scrupulous accuracy of detail every instance of *numen* they thought they had observed and give it its appropriate label, so that when it was needed, it might be induced to function again. Within this plurality of little powers were several groups, no doubt clearly enough defined to ancient experts, but often very obscure to us. Thus, we do not know the nature and functions of the classes called Novensides and Indigetes, though modern conjectures concerning them are plentiful. We do, however, understand the name of the Penates, for it signifies "dwellers in the store-room" (*penus*), and so clearly enough explains itself as containing the little household deities who watched over the food-supplies of the household. On the other hand, a second group of domestic gods, the Lares, who were of some importance, for their worship extended beyond the houses and land of individuals, are extremely vague to us, and in antiquity they were much obscured by identifications with certain Greek figures of origin probably quite other than theirs.

But even in early times, there were some manifestations of *numen* large and imposing enough in their nature and varied enough in their activity to be ascribed to someone greater than a Vervactor or one of the Penates. The sky, considered not as the place where the sun, moon and stars are to be seen, but rather as the region of the weather, including that very impressive kind of weather, a violent Italian thunderstorm, evidently had a vast deal of *numen* in it. And it is visibly one, with no natural differences to mark off one part of it from another. Therefore, like other speakers of the group of languages to which most European tongues belong, the Romans had one great sky-god, Juppiter, the last two syllables of whose name are simply the title "father", while the first is etymologically equivalent to the name of the Greek sky-god Zeus. Corn, again, is one kind of useful product of the earth, though there are different species of it, as wheat, barley and so forth, for they all alike serve for food, and indeed the principal food of the ancient Italian peasantry, who ate no great amount of meat as a rule. So not only the Romans but the Italians generally worshipped one great corn-deity, Ceres. They knew, of course, as well as we do that different soils will produce, or are best suited to produce, different sorts of edible plants, but the getting of food out of the ground was all the result of the same kind of *numen*, therefore one great source of *numen* was active. As to why they concluded that that source was female, even their sluggish imaginations seem to have been active enough to catch the resemblance between a fertile woman and a fertile field, which is so thorough a commonplace to the quicker-witted Greeks that it found its way into the formula with which an Athenian girl was betrothed. It is one of the few exceptions to the rule that they were quite incurious concerning the sort of persons their gods might be, provided always that their *numen* could be got to work for their worshippers when needed.

I say "when needed", because there is no evidence that Roman cult was ever the continuous thing which various types of Oriental worship, including some of the best-known forms of Christianity, are or have been. The gods lived in their holy places, and as time went on, it became the custom (it had not originally been so) to build them houses, albeit for the most part of foreign style ; there is no such thing as a Roman fashion of making what we call a temple, but they adopted first the Etruscan and then the Greek method of building and orienting one. The deities' presence was commonly made known to worshippers by signs or emblems of some sort, such as the Juppiter-stones of the Capitol and, even more curious, for the stones may well have been real or supposed meteorites, and therefore naturally connected with the *numen* of the sky-god, by the bundles of herbs which were known as "heads of gods" and used to represent them at certain old ceremonies. Later, again, the foreign fashion of having images in human shape in the temples was adopted, though not universally approved, for the dislike of images in worship is not a phenomenon confined to Protestant Christianity. But apparently all this divine apparatus remained unused for most of the time in the case of most deities ; Vesta is something of an exception, for her fire had to be continually kept going, and apparently a certain amount of other housework was performed in her shrine. But Mars, for example, or Quirinus, seems to have been left very much to himself in normal times between one festival and the next, provided no emergency occurred which called for a use of his particular kind of *numen* or for a general appeal to all the gods to avert or cure an evil, or again a general public thanksgiving to them all for some great benefit. In such cases, the shrines would be thrown open and citizens would visit them with humble prayers, the women, as with many peoples, being often the most zealous. The name of such an occasion itself means "a bowing down" (*supplicatio*).

What did go on daily was the domestic cult, kept up in all ages in every decent house throughout the Roman dominions. We do not know by any means all the details of this, but a fair amount of information has come down to us from a variety of sources, enabling us to patch together a picture not too untrue to ancient life. We may begin with the Lares. One of them came, how early we do not know, to be known as the Lar of the household (*Lar familiaris*), and we have what purports to be first-hand information as to how these deities felt the family should treat them. In the *Aulularia* of Plautus, the play from which Molière took, or rather adapted, the plot of *L'Avare* and the character of Harpagon, the prologue is spoken by the Lar. He informs the audience that for two generations he has been the guardian of a treasure buried under the hearth by the grandfather of the house's present owner, a miserly man called Euclio, the son and grandson of misers.

> "He has one daughter. Every day she prays,
> Bringing me incense, wine or other gift,
> And garlands ; so for this her piety,
> I have revealed the hoard to Euclio,
> To make a marriage-portion for the girl,
> Because a high-born youth has done her wrong."

Of the Penates something is said in that ode of Horace which was mentioned on p. 20. The good country-woman there garlands them with rosemary and myrtle ; at the first of every month she makes formal prayer, presumably to all the deities of her household, raising her hands palm upwards towards the sky, the regular ancient gesture on ordinary occasions. She also is dutiful towards the Lares, if indeed, for Horace is not an expert on religious matters and the two classes of godlings were often mixed, he does not mean the Penates, or the gods of the house generally, again. At all events, she gives them offerings of corn and wine and occasionally a pig, probably a sucking-pig. The great and expensive sacrifices of cows and bulls are not for her, nor for domestic cult generally, and from what we know of ancient sacrifices it is safe to say that the pig, after the proper portions had been given to the friendly little deities, formed the staple of the family dinner.

For gods and men shared the same meals in a Roman household. The table at which the human inhabitants of the house dined was in itself a holy thing, having, it would appear, its own share of *numen*. At all events, several acts of innocent native magic, or worship, for the line between the two was never very clearly defined, are connected with it. Plutarch, who was much interested in Roman ritual, tells us a little about this.

"Why," he asks in his *Roman Questions*, "did they not allow the table to be taken away empty, but insisted on something remaining upon it ?" and after some vague guesses as to amiable and moral reasons which might have originated this custom, but certainly did not, he finds very nearly the true one, "because no holy place should be left empty, and the table is holy".

Certainly the table is holy, as already stated. Therefore it is not well to leave it empty, for that is, or may easily be, a piece of sympathetic magic of quite the wrong kind, hunger-magic, tending to make it permanently empty, or at least bare of wholesome and satisfying food ; "when he takes food, may he not be able to eat it nor lessen his hunger" says an ancient curse in the Oscan dialect which someone's hatred has preserved to us, written on a piece of lead and deposited in or near a tomb for the ghosts and other uncanny powers to fulfil it. So it is best always to leave something, perhaps a loaf of bread or some *puls*, a sort of porridge which Roman country folk ate, standing upon it at all times, to let its *numen*, or that of the household gods, work useful, full-table magic, that the family may always have enough to eat. Those who wait or sit at it (the Greek fashion of reclining at meals on a sort of sofa is not native to Rome, though it was adopted later) should be clean people ; Juvenal waxes very indignant at persons of filthy life being allowed to come near it. When the family gathered for the principal meal of the day, a little of the food was set apart, in a small plate it would seem, for the gods, and at the end of the dinner a boy would get up, take it to the fire which burned upon the little family altar (or, doubtless, in older and simpler times, to the hearth which was kept alight under the smoke-hole in the roof), throw it in, and formally announce, amid the reverent silence of the rest, that the gods were favourable (*di propitii*). After that the dessert, or, as they called it, the "second tables" was brought in. This was rather an indulgence than a meal, and seems to have had no ritual attached. The table might also be the centre of a grave omen. For food to fall from a diner's hand onto the floor was always an unwelcome sign, but especially if a pontiff was taking a formal meal. The exact meaning of the sign was determined by what the person who let the food fall was saying or thinking of at the time, and strenuous measures were taken to avert ill consequences, for the floor under a table is the regular haunt of houseless and friendless ghosts, who have no one to provide the proper soul-feasts for them but, being miserable and hungry, are ill-tempered and apt to do mischief. So the food must be picked up and laid on the table again, without blowing the dust off it, thus pretending that it had not fallen, or bringing it once more into contact with the *numen* of the table, perhaps a little of both. Lastly, it was cast into the Lares' fire, thus leaving them to deal properly with it and remove it from the world of ghosts altogether. Pliny is our authority for this custom, which was obsolete or nearly so when he wrote (the principate of Vespasian, A.D. 69-79), as is shown by his use of past tenses in describing it. It belongs, then, to the old days, when the concept of *numen* was likely to be strong.

Vesta the hearth-goddess was herself one of the Penates in a way, at least very closely associated with them, but we know little of her private cult. It seems to have been the duty of the housewife to see that the hearth was clean every night before she went to bed, and to judge by the public cult, of which we shall have more to say later, the daughters of the house, if there were any, performed such simple and every-day rites as were called for. Vesta was never a purely ritual object or an imaginary figure. Fire is too obviously useful for that, and Vesta, in any Roman house of old days, before the more complicated modern domestic architecture came in (houses, under the Empire, if they belonged to well-to-do people, were much more modern and convenient than anything Europe was to see again until well into the nineteenth century), was nothing else than the ordinary fire used for cooking and heating. It burned on a hearth towards the back of the main room (originally the only room), the *atrium*, and on the opposite side, that towards the road or street, appeared the visible presence of another deity, almost exclusively Roman, Janus.

The name of Janus is connected with *ianua*, which means the outer door of a house. As a common noun, it signifies a gate or barbican, such as gave entrance to and exit from a walled place like Rome or any other considerable town in the ancient world. The name for the whole structure, in common parlance, was *porta*, but *ianus* was used in two ways, besides being the name of the god. It could mean a large double gate standing free, a not uncommon monument in classical times, comparable, as an ornament of the city, to such erections as the Marble Arch in London. There was, for instance, a *ianus geminus*, or two-arched gateway, in the Cattle Market (*Forum Boarium*) at Rome, and a still more famous one in the Forum proper, the administrative and commercial centre of the city under the Republic and later. But it could also mean one of the archways in an ordinary gate in the city wall. So, when the clan of the Fabii undertook their heroic, if legendary, single-handed campaign against the people of Veii, which ended in their destruction by superior numbers of the enemy, they marched forth, says Livy "by an unlucky route, the right-hand *ianus* of the Gate of Carmentis". That gate faced almost due south, therefore anyone going through it out of Rome was going as near as the structure would let him to the unlucky quarter, the west, if he took the right-hand opening. We shall have something to say later concerning right and left hand in Roman divination. But Janus was also present in every house, for naturally it must have a door of some kind, however simple. Now to go through a door, whether inwards or outwards, is to begin something, and beginnings are heavily charged with magical significance, in fact with *mana*, the world over. Hence it is not to be wondered at that the opening which let the Roman into or out of his home was laden with *numen*, which took to itself a name, that of the god Doorway. Nor is it very strange that in any full-length litany which addressed itself to all powers, small and great, Janus had first place, taking precedence even of Juppiter, while Vesta came last of all. It was simply what everyone saw when he came home, first the entrance to the house, then any objects which might be in the *atrium*, then the hearth-fire burning steadily (people who have no quick means of lighting a fire do not let it go out if they can help it) at the back of the room. So important, indeed, was the entrance-door that even its parts tended to assume a *numen* of their own. Once man gets beyond building a mere hut, of reeds or other material, and constructs a solid dwelling of timber or stone, his outer door will consist of two upright posts, a threshold, a lintel, and the door proper, swinging on hinges or, as was often the case in antiquity, revolving on a pivot. Of these the threshold is often the most substantial part, being in many cases a heavy block of stone, high enough to keep mud and water from coming into the house in bad weather. It may have been priestly elaboration which decreed that this part of the structure had two presiding deities, Limentinus and Lima, the god and goddess of the threshold (*limen*), But it is no theory, priestly or other, but fact that the actual threshold was an object of considerable importance. The bride, in Rome as in many places, was lifted over it as she entered her husband's house for the first time. We know well enough why, for Catullus, in one of his two marriage-songs, tells us ; it was for the omen's sake, lest she should stumble. But others let us know that there was more in it than that, for she also must not tread on it. Furthermore, she must win the favour of the entire doorway, and to that end she anointed the door-posts before she entered. The proper unguent was wolf's fat, for the wolf is not only a formidable but also a holy beast in Roman tradition ; it is Mars' own creature. Therefore so important a part of it as the fat would be heavily charged with *numen*. One would like to be told how hunters in early days dealt with a creature at once so troublesome in wild country and so sacred ; that they killed it out of hand, with no appropriate ritual, is simply incredible, but our authors date from times when Italy was for the most part well settled and tolerably policed, at all events in the territory originally Roman. However, wolf's fat naturally grew harder and harder to obtain, and later ages were content with hog's lard, again an important part of a beast closely connected with ritual and also with the idea of fertility, the blessing most wanted in marriage by the practically-minded peasants who started the custom going, or even common olive oil. The bride also fastened wool to the posts, another lucky substance.

But to return to the threshold, we have further evidence of its importance. Plautus has given us a scene in which a young man is leaving home, as he thinks, for ever. He is supposed to be an Athenian, but, as usual in that author, the atmosphere is completely Roman. He takes his solemn farewell of the supernatural powers, and his words are :

"Lintel and threshold, greetings, and fare you well. To-day, for the last time, I step outside my home and my country. . . . *Penates* of my father and mother, Lar master of our household, to you I confide my parents' affairs, to guard them well. I seek other *penates* and another Lar, another city, another country".

It hardly needs further proof that these parts of the prosaic house-door were charged with *numen* for a pious Roman of that day, about the end of the third or beginning of the second century B.C.

It has already been mentioned that the floor of the house was the haunt of uncanny presences, and we happen to know what was done to clear them out. For some reason, May 9th, 11th and 13th was an unlucky time of year, when ghosts were especially on the prowl. It was not the season when the family dead were honoured, for that was February, but the time for dealing with the houseless spirits. To do so was the task of the householder ; it was not a public rite performed by State experts, like those which we shall deal with in the next chapter. The ritual was gone through at midnight, when the officiant rose and went barefoot about the house, thus, in the old-fashioned and simple dwelling, remaining the whole time in contact with the earth, for the floor would be nothing else until later and more civilised ages. Making a magical sign to keep unholy things at arm's length, he then took nine black beans into his mouth ; beans, perhaps because they are apt to cause flatulence, are somewhat suspicious food to the ancients (in the Greek world, Pythagoreans would not eat them), and a popular idea seems to have been that they are connected with ghosts and the realm of darkness generally. At all events, they are not uncommonly ghosts' diet. These he would drop or spit out, saying as he did so, "With these I ransom me and mine". It was supposed that the ghosts (*lemures*) followed him and picked up and ate the beans, thus rendered more attractive by having something of the flavour of man from being in a live man's mouth. But he was very careful not to turn his head to see them do it, a precaution regularly taken by the officiant in any religious or magical ceremony which brings him in contact with dangerous powers. Finally, he dismissed his undesirable guests with as little offence to their feelings as possible. He washed his hands, clanged together some sort of bronze or copper objects—probably an ordinary cooking-pot would serve his turn, for the point of it was to make a metallic sound, which spirits do not like—and finally said "Good Folk (*manes*, the polite name for the dead), get you gone".

If we pass from the floor of the house to its roof, we still find evidence that the supernatural had its part. Roman houses had no such elaborate means of getting rid of smoke as our chimneys. In the roof of the *atrium* there was a square opening, the *impluuium*, literally "rain-in place", which served at once to collect rain-water in a tank placed underneath and to let out the fumes from the hearth-fire. We have some evidence that this was on occasion the way in and out for other than normal or mortal visitants. If a man was abroad and falsely reported dead (for instance, a soldier missing on active service), he had a fairly elaborate ceremonial to go through on his return. For, having been declared dead, he officially belonged to the other world, and not to this ; his relatives, we gather from Plutarch, who is our informant here, would have celebrated his funeral rites, thus making him over to the abode of ghosts. Therefore it was not fitting, as our author justly remarks, that he should use the front door, which we have seen to be a holy thing. He must climb up on the roof and let himself down by a rope through the *impluuium*. What else he did in order to restore himself to the communion of the living, we do not know ; the thorough-going and logical Greeks in like case made him go through the form of being a baby again, that being the recognised pathway into normal human life, but there is no direct evidence for such a performance in the Roman area, though in itself it is not unlikely. As to the use of the opening in the roof as the way out for unchancy things, we have the case the priest of Juppiter, who was so holy that nothing unlucky was tolerated in his presence. Therefore, if a man in bonds managed to get into his house, he must at once be loosed, and the fetters be flung out through the *impluuium*, lest they pollute his doubly sacred doorway. There is a certain amount of evidence that the roof is, not only in ancient Rome but at various times and places, a place where things not of this world may be expected to come and go.

Enough has perhaps been said to make it clear that no small amount of *numen* existed in the ordinary dwelling-house of early Rome. But most of the population lived, not in the City itself, but somewhere in the territory surrounding it, and got their living by tilling the land or raising cattle, especially the former, since Italians were and are no great meat-eaters. It was not to be expected that the fields should be destitute of *numen*, since we have seen that it existed in such familiar objects as the boundary-marks dividing them. It was the care of every farmer to draw around his land a magic circle, shutting out evil and shutting in good. Several writers tell us something of the circumambulation of the fields (*Ambarualia*), none more charmingly than Tibullus, who, like his greater contemporary Vergil, was country-bred and had an affection for the old ways. What follows is largely a prosaic paraphrase of his pretty verses in the first poem of his second book, but with a detail or two added from elsewhere.

The first requisite was "good words". By this neither Tibullus nor anyone else who wrote in Latin meant pious remarks nor prayer-formulae only, though doubtless both would be in place. It was rather the avoidance of ill-omened words, for in Latin as in many tongues *nomen omen*, a name, or indeed any significant word, "means something", often much more than it says. Thus, in calling up men for the armed forces, it was customary to call first someone whose name had welcome associations ; a man whose personal name was Kaeso, "slasher", or whose family surname was Victor, for example, would certainly find himself well up in the list. So in this country rite, everyone would avoid, during the ceremony, any such remark as "this field ought to do well if we don't have another drought this year". It is no great wonder that those concerned usually kept as quiet as they could (the Greek verb which signifies "to say good words", *euphemein*, commonly means "to be silent", and a like secondary meaning attaches to the equivalent Latin phrase *fauere linguis*, "to be lucky with tongues"), except while repeating the words of the sacred litanies, which would be dictated to them, slowly and audibly, by the local expert. Next, no work must be done, not only all human inhabitants of the farm but the draught-cattle enjoying a holiday and oxen as well as men and women being crowned with garlands. These were no mere ornaments, but rather magical objects, composed of plants supposed to be lucky or well-pleasing to the gods concerned, which would thus protect the head and consequently the whole person against evil influences while at the same time instilling good ones. Later casuists exercised some ingenuity, reminiscent of that shown by Jewish rabbis in deciding what constitutes "work" and therefore a violation of the Sabbath, to make clear what, if anything, a farmer might do on a holy day. But the people concerned are not said to be idle ; rather they are busy, *operati*, at their task, which on this day is not ploughing or weeding but getting a supply of good influences, in fact of the right kind of *numen*, for their land. Thirdly, everyone must be pure, *castus*. This included sexual purity, no one being allowed to take part who had indulged his natural appetites the night before. Hence, with the growth of a moral meaning in what was originally a purely ritual word, the modern sense of "chaste" ; but to begin with there was no ethical feeling attached to it. The participant in such a rite would need all the *numen* that was to be had, and sexual relations are full of *numen*, therefore to engage in them would use up the available supply of that precious power. Equally a part of the ritual purity is the wearing of clean white clothes and a formal washing in running water, from a spring or stream. An altar would be set up, if there was no permanent one, but if there was, it would be prepared for use by having a green turf laid on top of it. The victim (Tibullus specifies a male lamb, and no doubt this was a very common choice) was then led three times around the land, followed by the farmer and all his people, in their white clothes and wearing wreaths of olive. This was one of the most appropriate materials for such a purpose. Trees which bear useful fruit are lucky (the word *felix*, which is applied to such a tree, means primarily fruitful and secondarily fortunate), and the olive is the most valuable of all in the Mediterranean region, where it is the primary source of the carbohydrates necessary to any balanced diet. Butter is its Northern substitute, and the synthetic preparations which eke out an insufficient butter-supply are the substitute for a substitute. The procession over, the victim was sacrificed, the act being accompanied by a prayer, as was always the case. A sacrifice (cf. p. 18) increases the *numen* of the god to whom it is given, and it is clearly of little use to do that unless the power concerned is told, in unambiguous terms, exactly what use his worshippers expect him to make of his heightened vigour. The gods of a legalistic people are naturally legalistic themselves, apt to keep to the letter of a contract. In this case the chief powers concerned are Bacchus (Tibullus means, or at least his ancestors would have meant, the Italian wine-god, Liber pater) and Ceres, and they are asked to give increase and keep all evil away. When the victim was killed, the next thing was to examine its entrails, especially the liver, for omens. If these were favourable, that is to say if the internal appearance of the beast was normal, it meant that the gods had accepted the offering and might be relied on to do their part, if nothing untoward happened in the meanwhiie. When their portions of the victim were prepared and burned on the altar-fire, all concerned could sit down with a good conscience to the feast which was regularly part of such a rite. Tibullus concludes his poem with a brief address to his patron Messalla and a long eulogy of the rural gods, which, for he is a poet of love, shades off into an account of the love-god's activities in the countryside. All this may very well represent the traditional hymns which we know were sung on such an occasion, for he is not writing a scientific or technical account of how to conduct the ceremony, but handling his theme with an imaginative writer's freedom.

It was not only on the occasion of this formal drawing of the magic circle that Roman farmers performed religious ceremonies in connexion with their land. The Lar familiaris has already been mentioned (p. 27). His brethren were out in the fields. Roman land was regularly distributed to its owners or tenants in a sort of chequer-board pattern of squares subdivided into squares. The whole was apparently a particular application of the principle of the *templum* which must be discussed more fully later (p. 85), but for the present this much will suffice. The surveyor of the parcel of land to be assigned to Roman colonists or other future holders of the region in question took up his position at some convenient central spot. He then sighted by means of a simple instrument called a *groma* (an Italian corruption of Greek *gnomon*, a pointer) along two main lines, one approximately north and south, the other roughly east and west, so as to form a great Greek cross. These lines were called, one the *cardo*, the other the *decumanus*, though which was which was a disputed point. Now it was a simple matter to complete a quadrilateral in which the cross was inscribed, and the resulting four parts could be subdivided again and again by the same method until the minimum unit desired was reached. Thus each tenant was presented, normally and ideally at least, with a square holding, forming a larger square with three adjoining allotments. Between them would be left little strips of un-tilled land, on the lines of the local *cardo* and *decumanus*, which might serve as paths, and the central point where these met, the place where a corner of each of the four properties almost touched, was called a *compitum*, or cross-roads. Here it was customary to set up a little chapel of the Lares of the cross-roads, *Lares Compitales*, open in all four directions, so that the Lar of each farm might have free ingress and egress to the common shrine. Before each open-ing, fifteen Roman feet away, stood an altar, whereon sacrifice might be made by each of the proprietors concerned to his own Lar, at a kind of harvest-home festival, the Compitalia, which down to very late times was held on no rigidly fixed day but simply when winter came and the round of farm-work was over for the time being ; early January was the usual season. Each farmer brought his plough and hung it up before the Lares, and there was feasting and jollity for him and his family. On the evening before, a curious ceremony was gone through, which puzzled the ancients themselves, as its meaning had clearly been forgotten. A woollen doll was hung up for every free member of the household, and a woollen ball for every slave. Antiquaries explained that these were substitutes for the human beings concerned and it was hoped that the Lares, or a goddess called Mania ("the good lady", a euphemism for an underworld power connected with the dead, *manes*) would take these and leave the living alone. This, however, like some modern theories of similar nature, arises from a common confusion. The Lares are powers of the earth, who among other things help it to be fertile ; but ghosts and the vague and grim gods who rule over them are also of the earth, for there the dead are buried. Hence the frequency with which ghosts are expected to help the tiller of the soil and on the other hand the kindly powers who do help him are dreaded because of the uncanny place in which they live. The truth probably is that the woollen dummies were put where the Lares could give them some of their own *numen*, just as various objects, including ornaments worn in childhood (a Roman boy carried a locket, *bulla*, with a little charm inside it, to protect him until he came to man's estate), used to be hung up before the Lar familiaris, that he might extend his protection through them to the persons they belonged to, and such things as hair were very commonly offered to all manner of deities for a like reason. The *numen* which had thus, as it were, soaked into the doll or ball representing each individual would stand him in good stead when he resumed work on the soil which the Lares protected and strengthened. Why mere lumps of wool stood for the slaves and more or less recognisable human effigies for the free persons, we do not know. Possibly the reason lies in the terminology of Roman law. A doll, however roughly made, must have some sort of head ; head is *caput* in Latin, and the word also means legal personality. But a slave is not a person in law, he has no *caput* in that sense, therefore perhaps it was felt that a headless thing, although made of a lucky material, was a better representative. of him. Incidentally, if the above explanation of the puppets is the true one, it is an instance of what we find very commonly in early religion and magic, namely that the *mana* which is handled and directed is no immaterial thing, like the "spiritual grace" of much later and more developed cults, but material, which can be absorbed like water in a woollen ball, or put into a boundary-stone by setting it in a hole which has consecrated things, the remains of a sacrifice, at the bottom.

As to the original meaning of the name Lares, we are, as often, reduced to guessing. A plausible guess starts from the oldest form of the name, which was Las, plural Lases (*s*, in old Latin, changed to *r* between vowels), and this suggests the first syllable of the adjective *lasciuus*, "playful". They may have been the merry or jolly godlings who like to see all go well on the land and everybody full-fed and happy. Certainly this fits the pictures of them which we see in Pompeian houses, for instance, since these show them dancing and holding drinking-horns, but we do not know how old the idea is which these pictures embody; the earliest Roman cults had no imagery at all, either painted or in the round.

A good deal of Italy was and is but ill-suited for cultivation, so beyond the farming districts stretched untilled land, much of it wooded. This, like all such territories, was haunted, and some attention must be paid to the powers dwelling in it. These were especially the Fauni and Faunae, whose names probably mean the Favourable Ones, an appellation much like those by which fairies are known in Great Britain and Ireland ("Good neighbours", "Good people" and so forth). Their number and personality were of the vaguest, and often we get the singular, Faunus. He had his festival in country districts, on December 7th, when the people of the *pagus*, or rural district, kept holiday with dances and suchlike occupations. Hardly more definite was Silvanus, He of the Forest (*silua*), another inhabitant of the wilder parts of the country. He lived so far from the town that he never came into any official State calendar, nor had a temple or priest in Rome; but the people whose cattle pastured in his region evidently thought it well to keep on good terms with him, and his dedications, chapels and statues found their way into the city in time, after long dotting the countryside. It is not unlikely that he contributed two saints to the Christian calendar, for it was not uncommon to call him *sanctus*, "holy", as all deities were, and to make his nature doubly clear by adding the adjective *siluester*, "of the forest" to his name. Hence SS. Silvanus and Silvester may be the offspring of a misread dedication belonging to pre-Christian cult.

Thus the farmer, by simple and time-honoured rites, strove to secure for his house and land the necessary *numen* and to keep away the wrong kind of *numen*, such as ghosts and fairies might be supposed to possess. His religion expressed itself in ceremonies performed by his family alone, by himself and his immediate neighbours (the Compitalia) and by the village or rural community (Paganalia). It is interesting to see how he met the crises of individual life, birth, marriage and death.

Birth, if we will believe the official records, was surrounded by a crowd of godlings who, presumably, helped the great goddess of women, Juno, in her attendance on the mother. Lucina, when that is not a title of Juno herself, made the baby see the light (*lucem*) for the first time. Whether the little goddess who performed this one simple act, or the great one who included that among her other activities, was the earlier we have no means of determining. Levana was present when the father or his representative picked up the baby from the ground, thus acknowledging it as his and undertaking to rear it. Candelifera was there to watch over the light which always burned in the birth-room ; and so on, almost without limit. But there was one little group which was rather more real and less to be suspected of being the creation of some theoriser. A woman in childbed is doing a thing which can still appear wonderful, if any capacity for wonder is retained, to the best-informed modern, however much he knows of the physiology of reproduction, and to an early Italian it must have been clear that *numen* was present. Now, the world over, the hostile powers hate fertility, and injure it and fertile persons and things if they can. But they also hate, at least the Italian ones did, evidence of the normal activities of mankind, such as ordinary housework, which indeed even the benevolent deities seem to dislike, for the everyday tasks of spinning and so forth were not done on feast-days. So the mother was protected by those homely means. When her baby was born and had been laid on the ground (to receive *numen* from Mother Earth, or perhaps to get his soul from the same source), picked up again and attended to (there was, according again to officialdom, a little goddess Cunina who looked after the child in the *cunae*, that is the cradle), three people were set to work guarding the house all night against the uncanny things from outside (some said that Silvanus was likely to come and make trouble). One of them chopped at the threshold—we have seen that it was heavily charged with *numen*—with an axe, one pounded it with a pestle, as if he were pounding corn on it, the third swept it with a besom. From these actions there sprang three minor deities, Intercidona, Pilumnus and Deverra, i.e., Cut-in-Two, Pounder and Sweeper. How much the country people believed in their existence we do not know, nor does it greatly matter ; in such cases a name is not of primary importance, for we have no evidence that anyone prayed to them, and it is in prayers and charms that it is essential to have the right name. But they certainly continued to use this piece of magic late enough for the authors we have to learn of it and record it.

The child, once past babyhood and able to understand what was going on, was himself, or herself, something of a sacred person. Boys, as already stated, wore a little locket containing a lucky object, probably a phallus, which scares away evil things, and also, when in full dress, did not use the plain white outer garment of their elders but a *toga praetexta*, a cloak with a purple fringe or hem. Magistrates also wore it, and the reason was the same ; the boy and the magistrate had certain sacral duties. The magistrate had to perform or take part in sundry religious rites in his official capacity ; the boy was an acolyte (in Latin *camillus ;* his sister was a *camilla*) to his father in the performance of the family rites. We know little of the details, but we have seen (p. 29) that a son of the house made the daily offering after dinner to the domestic gods, and we can guess from the public cult of Vesta (cf. p. 53) that the little girls helped their mother to tend the hearth and honour its goddess.

Marriage, in Roman ritual, has all its three parts well developed. If a woman is to marry into another family, still more into another clan, as was the usual rule in Rome, at least in early days, she must be severed from her own group, and therefore from its gods. But the gods may feel injured at losing a worshipper ; therefore it is well to show a little seemly reluctance at going away. Hence the show of violence to a Roman bride, who was torn from the arms of her mother, a business in which it used to be fashionable to see a relic of supposed primitive times in which wives were got by kidnapping ; better acquaintance with the history of the rite has shown us that there never was a time when that was the universal and respectable custom. Being so separated, and so no longer her father's daughter nor under the protection of the *numen* of his house and its gods, she is in a dangerous position, for she is not yet a wife and so has no husband to extend the protection of his *numina* to her. Therefore she must be very carefully guarded from head to foot, and Roman families took all possible precautions, in the most logical fashion, for all these customs are quite logical and rational, once the underlying assumptions are made. She wore, even in later times, an old make of under-garment known as a "straight smock" (*tunica recta*) ; in old days she would wear a *toga* over it, of the same fashion as her brothers' outer garments, but later this style went so out of use that to call a woman a "toga-wearer" in classical times meant that she was a prostitute ; respectable women wore a sort of long gown known as a *stola*. But her most conspicuous garment was her veil, made of yellow-dyed material, or sometimes red. Either colour was lucky, and thus her head and face were shielded ; the garment was called a *flammeum*. Her hair, which had previously been parted with a spear—ill-omened things cannot abide iron—was arranged in six locks, thus giving her a lucky number either side of her head, and wound with woollen ribbons or fillets. Like all persons engaged in business of religious importance, she had a wreath on her head, worn under the veil and composed of flowers and herbs gathered by herself. Thus she was well enough guarded against danger from above. Her waist was girdled with a woollen sash, tied in a particular style of knot, called, at least as far back as our information goes, the knot of Hercules. Behind her, and touching her, came not a bridesmaid but rather a bride's matron, a woman living in a first marriage, and so having about her none of the doubtful *numen* which would attach to widowhood (in early days there were no divorces). Front and sides were guarded by three boys, all of whom must have both parents living. One went before her, carrying a torch of whitethorn, a lucky material ; one held either arm. She herself carried a distaff and spindle, for the same reason, probably, as prompted the precautions taken at a birth (above, p. 41). Finally, to keep away all sounds of ill-omen and very likely to drown any charms an ill-wisher might recite, all the wedding-guests and everyone else who was there to look on joined in a shower of jokes, the broader the better, for indecent jokes are good magic, directed against bride and bridegroom, and also in shouts of *talassio*, a word so old that no one knew what it meant, except that it was the right thing to shout at a wedding. Nuts were thrown about, and the whitethorn torch (it seems to have been one of five torches, but we know nothing about the others) was thrown down, scrambled for and carried off. One of the reasons for this was that if husband and wife disliked each other, she could bring about his early death by putting it under the marriage-bed on the first night, and he hers by burning it at a grave.

On lifting the bride over the threshold (see p. 32), the third part of the marriage ceremony began. She had been severed from her father's house and brought safely through her period of temporary godlessness ; it remained to make her a wife. On her arrival, while she was still before the door of her future husband, she was asked, apparently by the bridegroom, who she was, and must answer with the puzzling formula : "Where thou art Gaius, I am Gaia". No one has ever satisfactorily explained these words, for a Roman wife did not take a new name. If she was, for instance, the daughter of a Fabius, her only legal name was Fabia, though she might have some personal name in her own home, for instance Tertia, or its diminutive Tertiola, if she was the third child.

and Fabia she remained all her life, married or not, though, if her husband was called Claudius, i.e., was a member of the Claudian family, she would be commonly known as "Claudius' Fabia" (*Fabia Claudii*) to distinguish her from other women of her original clan. The most likely suggestion is that Gaius is an old clan-name here, not a personal name, as it was in classical times, and that she meant "Whatever clan (or family) you belong to, I too belong to it henceforth", for that, in fact though not in name, a wife did. Be that as it may, measures were taken to assimilate her to her new household. After the ceremony at the door, she touched fire and water, the common materials of purification, thus burning and washing off her own strangeness, such remnants of the *numen* of her father's house as might cling to her, and any bits of bad magic she might have picked up on the way, and coming into contact with two essentials of life in any house. For that these things are fundamental and essential was a fact expressed elsewhere than in the marriage ceremony ; when a man was declared outlaw, the Roman formula was that he was excluded from water and fire, which henceforth none might share with him or let him have. In the *atrium* of the new house stood the bed of the Genius (*lectus genialis*), just opposite the entrance-door. It may have been originally the marriage-bed, for the oldest Roman house was one-roomed, but it remained in ritual use much later than this. That no human beings occupied it was a small matter, for its essential occupant was the Genius of the man or, as may have been the case, of his family. The word *genius* means "begetter", and personifies that particular kind of *numen* which enables the line to continue, generation after generation. This much we can still make out ; all else about the Genius is conjecture, for he is thickly obscured by confusion with a quite different Greek figure, the personal *daimon*.[1] It is possible that the sacred bed had another occupant. A Genius belongs to men ; there is some evidence that a woman had connected with her a sort of female counterpart to him, the Juno. However, the testimonies to the existence of this figure are none of them ancient enough for us to be at all sure that

[1] See *Ancient Greek Religion*, p. 144.

she belongs to the earliest stratum of Roman religion. But
the ceremonies we have described were not all that the bride
had to go through. She had with her three coins ; one of
these she handed to the bridegroom, one she laid before the
deities of the house, the third she took the next morning to
the nearest cross-road and offered it to the Lares Compitales
there. She was now, for the marriage was consummated on
the night of her arrival at her new home, a house-mother,
mater familias, and remained so whether she ever had children
or not.

While death was no more welcome in early Italy than
elsewhere, it does not appear that the native Roman belief,
or that of Italians generally, added to the natural shrinking
from it any extreme fear of the next world or of ghosts.
Archaeological evidence from the oldest sites suggest that
the living took no great pains to put elaborate barriers between
themselves and the dead, and stories of hauntings, though
they exist, are not common in classical Latin, and such as
there are concern chiefly the kind of ghost most likely to be
formidable, that of a person dead by violence and denied the
proper rites of burial. There were decencies to be observed,
and as usual these took the form of avoiding the wrong kind
of *numen*, for it can hardly be doubted that the dead, or the
powers of the world of the dead, were thought to exercise
some at least. When a death occurred, the household was for
the time being in a state of tabu or ill-luck, *funesta*, and
consequently observed a period of mourning. The first and
most obvious step to get rid of this undesirable state was to
transfer the departed from the world of the living to that
which was now his proper abode, the realm of the "good
people" (*manes*). Popular thought concerning this was apparently of the vaguest ; it is a disputed point whether there
was a native Roman god of the dead, corresponding to the
Greek Hades-Pluton. Nor was there ever much distinction
of individual dead people ; nothing remotely like Greek
hero-cult is native to Rome. The corpse, laid on a bier of
some kind, was washed, anointed, and, if that of a person
of any official position, dressed in the costume befitting his
rank ; we may conjecture that a common man was put into

ordinary decent attire, such as he might wear when going about his business or pleasure in life. The body was now taken to the burial-place, which might be somewhere on the land the living person had tilled, or in a suitable spot set apart for burials and cremations ; very often tombs were at the side of roads, and all manner of constructions for the reception of corpses or ashes were made from time to time, varying, according to the date, the standing of the deceased, and the amount of expense that was thought proper, from the simplest pit in the soil or rock to the most elaborate monument. The essential thing was that the body should be put under earth, and if for any reason the entire corpse was not so disposed of, at least a bone or some small portion, say a finger, cut off from the rest had a clod of earth formally laid upon it ; a man was buried, according to the findings of priestly experts, when no bone of him was above ground, and till then the period of mourning must last. Cremation was common, but by no means universal ; for example, the dictator Sulla was the first of his clan, the Cornelii, to be burned. But fire was a necessary thing, for all funeral processions carried torches, not, as some ancients and moderns after them suggested, because originally funerals were always at night, a proposition which has no real proof, but because fire or light or both are regular forms of protection against ill-luck and bad influences. The children and other kin of the dead followed the bier, and if cremation was used, the nearest relative lit the pyre, with his face turned away. The grave was in a sense in consecrated ground ; it was not a *locus sacer*, or dedicated spot, like the precinct of a temple, but *religiosus*, more or less strictly tabu, and not to be lightly approached. Certain rites, including the sacrifice of a pig, were proper in preparing it. The corpse being bestowed in whatever manner was preferred, the house from which the funeral procession started was purified by sundry rites, including a sacrifice to the Lares, and the period of strict mourning was concluded by the *nouendiale sacrificium*, the offering of the ninth day, i.e., by our count, eight days after the burial, for Latin generally reckons inclusively and says, e.g., that the tenth day of a month is four, not three, days before the thirteenth.

Such, in outline, was an ordinary funeral by native Roman rites, so far as we can reconstruct them ; a great many details remain obscure and need not be gone into here. Great families adopted, from quite early times, a much more elaborate funeral ceremony, which seems to be of Etruscan origin. In this, while the main and essential features were unaltered, the funeral procession was increased by a number of persons, including musicians, professional mourners, and, most remarkable and impressive of all, the visible presence of the ancestors of the dead. It was the custom of such families to decorate the walls of the *atrium* with wax masks of former members of the family. On the occasion of a death, these would be taken down and worn by actors who personated the earlier dead, wearing the robes of the highest office each had held and riding in vehicles appropriate to their rank. Thus a Roman noble would go to the world of the dead escorted by a long series of magistrates of the past, in full dress and sit.ing on their official seats mounted upon wagons. At a suitable place—in Rome, the Forum—a halt would be made while one of the family pronounced a speech in praise of the newly dead, and while the general rule was that no burial might take place within the city walls, certain families were exempt from that law, and in token of such privilege, for a moment held a torch under the bier, as if to cremate their kinsman on the spot. But all these and other elaborations, besides being much too expensive for the ordinary family, were quite inessential to the real business of getting the departed member of the family out of this life and into the next world. He was not neglected there, even after the nine days were over, but had his portion in the annual Feast of Souls (*Parentalia*, festival of parents, and so of ancestors generally), held in February, the usual month for rites of a dismal kind and for purifications. The State recognized, but did not conduct the soul-feast, for which nine days were assigned, the thirteenth to the twenty-first inclusive of the month, perhaps in imitation of the family's nine days of full mourning. The last of these is marked in the State calendars as the Feralia, but even it, according to our oldest authority on such things (see p. 52), was not barred to public business, while in the interval came two festivals of some importance, the Lupercalia and the Quirinalia, the only days of the whole series which were public holidays on which the courts did not meet and no legislative assemblies might be held. They were, however, days of ill omen for most things, for example no marriages were held then, the temples were closed and magistrates did not wear their purple-edged cloaks. These were decent and ordinary precautions to take while ghosts were about, watching their surviving relatives decorate the burial-places and otherwise attend to their wants ; but at the same time they indicate that ghosts, if properly treated, were not beings of whom any normal Roman went in panic fear, but simply senior members of Roman families, to be treated with the deep respect which every well-brought-up junior showed to his elders.

From this brief and imperfect sketch of the private cult of ancient Rome we pass to those forms of worship which were on a larger scale.

CHAPTER II

THE GODS OF THE ROMAN STATE

T H E rites of which we have hitherto spoken are generally called household ceremonies, *sacra domestica*. Not a few were celebrated by larger ur.its ; thus a clan might have ceremonials of its own to perform and kept them up sometimes under circumstances of great difficulty. Thus, it is said that when the Gauls occupied Rome all but the Capitol, in 390 B.C., one of the garrison was Gaius Fabius Dorsuo, a member of an old and noble house. The time came for certain rites to be performed by a member of his clan (*gens ;* the word included all free-born men who had the same surname, in this case Fabius), on the Quirinal Hill, and he undertook to perform them. Taking the necessary utensils and materials and clothed in the proper garb for such an occasion, he calmly went down from the Capitol, passed through the enemy's lines, paying no attention to their shouts and totally unafraid, reached his destination, did what was necessary, and came back again, "in good hopes", says Livy, who tells the story with his usual vividness, "that he had the favour of the gods, seeing that not even the fear of death could stop him serving them". Livy leaves us to decide for ourselves whether the Gauls were simply too dumbfounded by his boldness to do anything or awed by fear of the supernatural, "to which their race", he adds, "is somewhat prone".

There were other cults likewise, on behalf of portions, not the whole, of the State, and some of these we shall have occasion to mention in this chapter. There were likewise ceremonies kept up, by permission of public authority, by artificial associations, generally known as *collegia*, but these hardly belong to early days, since they are characteristically the resource of foreigners who have no share in the State cult, adherents of some non-Roman but tolerated religion, or slaves and other little people, who, having no kinsfolk or none of any social and economic standing, clubbed together to insure decent burial for themselves when they died and in the meantime a little social life. The normal Roman of early days was born into a whole complex of communities smaller than the State, his family, his *gens* or clan, his *curia* or subdivision of the people, his *tribus*, which was a division at once of the people and the land they lived on, often having the name of a clan, perhaps other groups as well, and so needed no artificial associations. Women were less prominent outside their own households, but were by no means excluded from the State's cult as a whole, still less from the *sacra* of groups within it to which they might belong by birth or marriage. There were some particular rites in which no woman might take part, others from which all men were excluded, but both sexes had their share in the great majority of cults.

Before trying to describe the Roman state cult in its earliest recoverable form, it is necessary to say a word about

the calendar, for many festivals of gods are fixed to particular
days of the year, although not all are ; official language spoke
of *feriae statiuae*, or fixed feasts, and *feriae conceptiuae*,
movable feasts, whose exact date was determined year by
year, usually within a more or less rigidly fixed period. The
oldest calendar was very imperfect, consisting of but ten
months, March to December, of which only the first four,
Martius, Aprilis, Maius and Iunius, had names (all the above
are adjectives, and *mensis*, a month, is to be supplied with
them), the rest being numbered, Quintilis, Sextilis, September, October, Nouember, December ; we still use the last
four names, generally forgetting that they mean respectively
the seventh, eighth, ninth and tenth month. The comparatively dead season between the end of one year's agricultural
work and the beginning of the following spring was not
reckoned ; a phenomenon not uncommon in early attempts
at counting days. Then someone, probably one of the
Etruscan kings who governed Rome before the days of the
Republic, introduced a better calendar, which for the first
time was an approach to a true year, for it was, or tried to
be, continuous. He added two months, Ianuarius, the month
of the festival of Janus, which he clearly intended to begin
the series, although it never did until much later, and
Februarius, the month of purification (*februa* are materials
used in ceremonies of purification and avoidance). In this,
the calendar which served the Republic till its last days, four
months (March, May, July, still called Quintilis, and October)
had 31 days each, the rest 29 except February, which had 28.
The total was thus 355 days, or roughly $10\frac{1}{4}$ days too few
to match the solar year ; the balance was approximately
redressed by inserting a short month, Intercalaris or Mer-
cedonius, between February 23rd and 24th. This additional
group of days numbered 22 or 23, and was supposed to be
inserted at such intervals as would bring the total number
back again to the beginning of a solar year ; in practice, the
clumsy arrangement was made worse by miscalculations,
accidental and deliberate (clearly, it would often be politically
convenient for one party or another to retain magistrates on
whose support they could depend for an extra three weeks

or more), and by Julius Caesar's time the official year was far astray of the real seasons. He stopped all pretence of lunar months, instituted a solar year of 365 days, and made its length nearly right by inserting one day where once the extra month had stood, thus repeating the date February 24th once every four years. But till his time, the months were supposedly lunar, and each had three main days in it, the Kalends, or time of proclaiming (what was proclaimed, on the day of new moon, was the length of time till the next named day), the Ides, which was the time of full moon, the fifteenth day of the four long months and the thirteenth of the others, and the Nones, i.e., the Nines, eight days, as we reckon, nine by Latin count, before the Ides, and so on the seventh day of a long month, the fifth of a normal one. All other days were expressed by saying that they were such-and-such a number before one of these dates, and of this reckoning a remnant survives in our own tongue, for the other name for leap-year is bissextile year, that is the year in which the sixth (*sextus*) day, counting inclusively, before the Kalends of March, i.e., February 24th, comes twice (*bis*).

This rather complicated arrangement was not generally known in times when reading was not common (though letters were never kept the secret or privilege of any particular class) and the rudiments of astronomical science were a very rare possession indeed. But in 304 B.C. the calendar was published, and at some time, we do not know exactly when, it became customary to set up in convenient places copies of it, annotated with the names of the fixed festivals and other matters of interest. One Republican specimen of these survives, the battered but precious Calendar of Antium (*Fasti Antiates*), from fairly early in the first century B.C., also several of Imperial date, conformed to Caesar's revision, but still giving an account of the festivals, sometimes with valuable annotations, the fruit of contemporary learning. Of these festivals, a number are inscribed in larger letters than the other entries; it is as certain as anything of the kind well can be that these are the oldest known, and from them we can form at least an outline idea of the early and comparatively pure Roman cult, before foreign ideas began to have much effect. Whether it is in our power to get back to a time of wholly Roman cult containing nothing but native elements is another matter ; it is far from certain that such a state of things existed, once that mixed settlement known as Rome had been founded.

Starting, then, with these oldest festivals, it is to be noted that a few of them are an extension to the State of the domestic worship we have already learned to know. Let us begin with the hearth. Whatever happened to other people's fires, there was one which must always have been carefully tended in a little early community, and that was the domestic fire of the chief or king. So long as that burned, there was a supply of fire for the whole people, and there is some reason for saying that it was in a sense an embodiment of the communal life, for life, light and fire are ideas closely conjoined in simple thought. So it is not to be wondered at that there was a public Vesta in Rome, and that her fire was tended by virgins, the successors of the king's daughters, whose official abode was close by the Regia, the building which replaced the old palace of the kings. There were six of these women in historical times, originally, it is said, four. They were chosen, while still little girls, from families of patrician origin, that is to say descended from original or early settlers of Rome, and they served for thirty years (originally it had been but five), during which time they must not marry. If one of them was found unchaste, she was not executed, for she was too holy to kill, but put into an underground chamber in the Field of Ill-luck (*Campus sceleratus*), and there left to die of hunger and lack of air, or be miraculously rescued, if Vesta chose thus to vindicate her innocence. It was an ordeal, not an execution. Her lover, if known, was beaten to death. Their service, which was one surrounded with high honours, was naturally concerned chiefly with Vesta herself, though they took part in sundry other rites as well. The ceremonial was complicated, and one account, probably owing not a little to gossip, says that a Vestal spent her first ten years in learning it, the next decade in practicing it and the third in teaching it to novices. That part of which the general public knew something was the tending of the holy fire, the extinction of which was a serious portent ; the Romans, says Dionysios of Halikarnassos, fear the worst if it happens, for they take it as a sign that their State shall be destroyed. We do not know exactly whence this learned Greek had his information, though it must have been from a good Roman source, but he probably has got to the root of the matter. The fire of Vesta was the hearth of the City and Empire, and a cold hearth is an uninhabited house in the feeling of most peoples. Sundry means of expiation were used, but the regular remedies included the beating of the Vestal responsible and the rekindling of the fire in the most primitive fashion, by friction of wood, which must be taken from a fruitful tree, and the lighted tinder carried to the hearth in a bronze sieve. Other rites included bringing water for Vesta's household uses ; it must not come from the regular water-supply of the City, when one was instituted, but from a sacred spring, that of Egeria, outside the Porta Capena, one of the southern entrances to Rome. Furthermore, it must not be set down on the way from the spring, lest its virtue should be lost by contact, even indirect, with the earth, and consequently the Vestals carried it in a vessel which had a narrow bottom and would overset if put on the ground. Another piece of sacred house-work was the preparation of the salt needed in ritual. This must all be done, it would seem, by the Vestals themselves. They started with the dirty product of a salt-pan, which they then pounded in a mortar, baked in a jar, and (presumably after some process of cleaning, by dissolving and filtering it) reduced finally to a hard lump, which when wanted was cut up with an iron saw ; one of several proofs that the cult of Vesta, as we know it, is not one of the oldest in Rome, for we shall see later that bronze is the ancient sacral metal. To make *mola salsa*, that is to say salted grain or flour, one of the commonest offerings, they prepared their own corn ; the three senior Vestals would gather, between May 7th and 14th, but only on the odd-numbered days, such ears of spelt as were by that time to be found ripe, which they then brought back with them, threshed and ground or pounded, and on three occasions in the year mixed with the prepared salt, a supply of which they kept in the shrine. These occasions were the feast of Vesta herself, June 9th, the Lupercalia of February 15th, and the Banquet of Juppiter (*Epulum Iouis*) on September 13th, an instance of their activity in other rites than those of their own goddess. Vesta, always represented by her own hearth-fire and never by an image, was housed in a small round building in the Forum, which although in our use of the word it was a temple, for it was devoted to sacral uses, was not one in the Roman sense, for it did not stand upon ground formally set apart for the use of the gods after proper consultation of the omens. It contained, besides the holy hearth, the storeroom, in which were kept a number of objects too holy ever to be seen save by the goddess's own priestesses, and therefore of unknown nature, though conjectures as to what they were bore testimony to the ingenious curiosity of not a few Roman antiquaries. The theory most in favour was that they included the Palladium, the sacred image of Athena which had been the "luck" of Troy, and was said to have been stolen from her temple there by the Greeks before they took the city. This, however, was no part of Roman tradition, but belonged to a pseudo-historical Greek theory, which, if a non-Greek people showed any signs of being civilised, was prone to declare them descendants of the worthiest opponents of Greek heroes, and so discovered that Rome had been founded either by Aeneas or by some descendant of his.

If Vesta had her place in State cult, so had the Penates. We have seen that her shrine had a store-room, *penus*, and that seems to have been their abode, as the *penates* of a private house kept watch over the more commonplace stores in the larder. Here again fancy was hard at work, and identifications of these obscure gods, who yet were felt to be important, showed much ingenuity, but little knowledge of or regard for the facts of religious history. We need have little hesitation in saying that to begin with they were the guardians of the royal store-cupboard, which no doubt was a somewhat larger and more imposing thing than that of an ordinary family, though we need not suppose it was very magnificent, for the original Roman kings were the chiefs of a small community which still had a long way to climb on the ladder leading to civilisation. So we may think of the round shrine, the ruins of whose latest ancient reconstruction are still to be seen in the Forum, as a sort of annex to the king's house, the place where his daughters looked after the important hearth and the stores which he, or the queen, saw fit to keep there. There was still a trace of the old association of father and daughter left in historical times, although the Vestals were under the supervision of the chief pontiff when we hear of them. On certain occasions they used to go to the King of the Sacred Rites, the last survival of the sacral functions of extinct royalty, and solemnly ask: "Wakest thou, King? Be wakeful!" We do not know what these occasions were, but may perhaps glimpse through the little we know to an older time when the daughters of a real king used to summon their father for some piece of ritual which he and they had to perform together.

If the Holy Hearth was publicly honoured in Rome, the Holy Door was not forgotten. The *ianus* in the Forum has already been mentioned (p. 31), and there is no satisfactory proof that it was ever anything but a ceremonial gateway, independent of any system of fortification. It would appear that it was used for important war-magic. As already mentioned (*ibid.*), there was a right and a wrong way for an army to march out, and it seems probable that early Roman armies paraded formally through this gate, with precautions against doing so in any but a lucky direction, when they set forth on campaign. To make this an easier and quicker business, or merely to indicate that it was necessary, the *ianus* was open in wartime, and this, as Rome's political commitments expanded, meant that it was very seldom closed, since she was generally at war somewhere. Hence it is not strange that it came to be thought of as the gate of war, within which, on the rare occasions when peace reigned, War was imprisoned, to be let out when, at the outbreak of fresh hostilities, the gate was once more thrown open. In the case of other arches which bore the god's name, no such ceremonies seem to have taken place, and we do not know precisely what they were for, if it was not simply ornament.

Besides these deities of the house, the Lares had their place in the State cult. Since their shrines, when not in houses, were (p. 38) at cross-roads, it was no great extension to suppose them protectors of roads (*Lares uiales*), and so of those who travelled in any way, including seafarers (*Lares permarini*). Soldiers must march, therefore we know, though our information is not early, that on occasion the Soldiers' Lares (*Lares militares*) were addressed. In general, it seems to have been felt that these public Lares guarded the Roman land and its citizens much as the private ones looked after the farms and those who tilled them. Corresponding also to the ceremonial of the farm were certain rites, quite as much magical as religious, that is to say depending upon the mere performance of the ceremonial as much as on winning the favour of any god, for their efficacy.

We saw (p. 35) the Roman farmer drawing a magic circle about his lands at the Ambarualia. The indications that this was ever attempted for the territory of Rome, even in the oldest times, when it was but a few miles across, are faint and unsatisfactory, but a corresponding ceremony, the Amburbium, or circuit of the City, was used now and again ; Lucan tells us that it was tried by the Senatorial government in 49 B.C., when Caesar was on the march against them. But much older and more interesting was the very ancient ceremony of the Lupercalia (February 15th). By all accounts, Rome began as a little settlement on the Palatine Mount, a naturally strong position west of the Forum, which in early days was handy to the river and defended during a great part of the year by marshy ground about some at least of its circuit. The boundaries of this old village, for it cannot have been much more, followed roughly the contour of the foot of the hill, except towards the river, where they swung out to include the Cattle Market and the great altar of Hercules which protected traders there. This was what the Romans, perhaps then, certainly later, knew as the *pomerium* of their town, the sacred boundary, approximately following the line of the fortifications, hence its name, "behind-wall" or "wall-behind". In classical days it was still marked by a line of stones, for the old rite never ceased to be celebrated till the final triumph of Christianity. On the appointed day, two young men of good family made ready to play their parts. They met in a cave on the Palatine, the Lupercal, or Place of the Wolf. There a dog and some goats, perhaps two, were sacrificed, and the young men were daubed with blood, presumably that of the goats, which was then wiped off with wool, or perhaps goat's hair, dipped in milk. Then, naked except for a loin-cloth and carrying strips of goat's hide, they ran around the *pomerium* of the Palatine settlement, striking at everyone they met. Two interesting features of the ceremony are, that they were popularly called he-goats themselves, and that anyone, especially a woman, whom they struck was supposed to be delivered from barrenness.

The general sense of the rite is clear enough, although some details are obscure. The object of it is to trace a magic circle, thus shutting out evils, especially infertility, and shutting in good. This is done by the young men transforming themselves, for the time being, into human he-goats, the very embodiments of sexual vigour and at the same time of pugnacity. It is not by accident that the ancients supposed the performance to take place in honour of a god who might be identified with the Greek Pan, for he too is a he-goat, partly humanised. Besides infertility, another evil is to be excluded, the most dreaded of common European wild beasts ; the word Lupercus almost certainly means "averter of wolves", and a man who ran this holy course was called a Lupercus. But, and this is perhaps the most interesting point of all, no one gives us any clear and credible account of what god it was whom they thus honoured, or were supposed to honour, and it is very likely that the entire performance was pure magic, at least originally. The dog-sacrifice would serve to get the good will, or at least avert the hostility, of any uncanny powers who might lurk in the ground or the cave. The whole ceremony puzzled the Romans of historical times, and gave rise to some ingenious but unfounded theories, more than one of which has misled incautious modern enquirers.

Passing now to rites which certainly were in honour of gods, we begin with that one whose *numen* is perhaps most obvious of all, the great god of sky and weather, Juppiter.

The calendar seems to have been made and adopted too early for the most famous of his cults to be included. As Optimus Maximus, the best and greatest of all Juppiters, he had an imposing temple on the Capital, fronting south after the fashion of its Etruscan designers and having three chapels, the centre one for the god himself, while on either side were two female partners, Juno and Minerva. But the grouping is not native Italian, and in purely Roman cult Juppiter has quite other associations ; even a connexion with Juno is at least highly doubtful, and the etymology of her name is still too uncertain for anyone to say confidently whether or not she originally has anything to do with him. To worshippers with their minds full of Greek legends and popular identifications of Greek deities with their own, it was of course obvious enough ; Juppiter was Zeus, the Greek sky-god, Juno was Hera, his wife, and Minerva was Athena, his daughter. As a matter of fact the names Juppiter and Zeus come from the same original linguistic stock, Juno does much resemble Hera in her functions, and Minerva has something in common with Athena, for both are patronesses of craftsmen ; but, as has already been said, no Italian legend makes any deity the blood-relation of any other, and Rome, unprompted from outside, showed no inclination to associate these three holders of *numen*, of whom Minerva was not native, though she is Italian.

However, Juppiter was firmly fixed in the calendar, even though this one great cult was perforce omitted. All the Ides belong to him, for a very intelligible reason ; they are the days of full moon, or at least are supposed to be, and at full moon that very important piece of sky-*numen*, light, is displayed practically throughout the twenty-four hours if there are no thick clouds about. On the Ides of every month, a white wether was led along the Sacred Way, the old street which led into the Forum and was a regular processional route, up to the Capitol, and there sacrificed by Juppiter's own priest, the Flamen Dialis. Concerning this functionary something must now be said, for he represents a very ancient stratum in the complicated religious history of Rome. He had about him some of the outward marks of kingship, such as the right to be attended by a lictor, or bearer of the rods (and, outside Rome, axes) which marked the presence of a magistrate with coercive powers. He wore the dress of a magistrate, with its purple-edged toga ; his official seat, like that of a senior magistrate, was a special kind of chair known as curule (*sella curulis*). He had the right to be present at meetings of the Senate, which was originally the king's council. There are indications that his office went back to the royalty of the Bronze Age, for iron might not touch his person ; his hair and nails were cut with bronze implements. Quite possibly he was the result of some ancient political compromise, in which the king of an older bronze-using population was stripped of most of his secular powers by an iron-using people, but left with his sacral functions and treated with high respect as a holy person, belonging to the cult of a great god. Be that as it may, his entire life was devoted to the service of his deity, and not only his, but that of his household, for he must be married, and that by the most ancient rite of all, known as *confarreatio*, the central ceremony of which was the eating by bride and bridegroom of a cake made, not with wheat, but with the older and inferior grain known in English as spelt, Latin *far*. Such marriages, because they could not be dissolved otherwise than by the death of one of the parties, were rare in historical times. If his wife, the Flaminica, died, he must lay down his office, for the worship of Juppiter was not to be carried out by one person, but by a family. If there were no children, a substitute was furnished in boys and girls who had both parents living and acted as *camilli* and *camillae* (see p. 42). Apart from this, he was surrounded with a most extraordinary complex of prohibitions. Every day was a holiday for him, therefore he must not only do no work, but see none, and an attendant went ahead of him to warn anyone working to leave off till he was past. He must not come into contact with anything suggesting war, for which reason he might not see an election, for the voters assembled in their military divisions at the polls. Nothing resembling bonds must come near him ; even his ring must be cut through, or it would be too much like a fetter. We have already seen that a man in bonds was delivered if he got to the flamen's house (p. 34). This was carried so far that he might not pass under a trellis on which a vine was trained, for its tendrils suggested fastenings. He must always wear his *apex*, a kind of mitre, in the open air, that is in sight of his god, who must not see his priest otherwise than fully dressed. Even indoors, it was a comparatively late indulgence which allowed him to uncover his head, and to change his underwear he must go into some room which had no opening in its roof. Death must never come near him ; hence a funeral or any place where dead bodies were burned were forbidden to him. He must never mount a horse—another testimony to the antiquity of his office, for horses, other than native wild ones, are indeed long familiar in Europe, yet not so old-established that we cannot find traces of a time when they were new and therefore uncanny. A long list of unlucky or doubtful things must never be touched or even named by him, including a she-goat, uncooked meat, ivy, beans, meal which had yeast mixed with it, and dogs. It is therefore not surprising that slaves might not touch him ; his barber must be a free man. All possibility of evil magic was kept away, therefore he must not take an oath, for the ancient oaths regularly included conditional curses, in the form, "if I keep this oath, may good fortune befall me, but if not, ill-luck". Nor must such parts of his person as his hair-cuttings be left where an ill-wisher might find them, but carefully buried under a fruitful tree. He also must make a kind of pretence of sleeping on the ground, for the legs of his bed, from which he might never be absent for more than two nights, were daubed with mud. His wife also had numerous restrictions to observe, and herself conducted various ancient and holy rites.

But to return from the priest to the god, Juppiter, as befits a sky-god, had agricultural interests. These included the solemn business of inaugurating the vintage each year. At the Vinalia, or Feast of Wine, on August 19th, his *flamen* sacrificed a ewe-lamb, a curious victim, seeing that the usual rule is that the offering is of the same sex as the deity. After he had killed it, and before the sacrificial portions (*exta*) had been, after the Roman fashion, cooked and laid on the altar, the *flamen* solemnly cut the first bunch of grapes ; the vintage might then be carried on. Of other festivals of Juppiter we know little more than their dates, though concerning one, which came on December 23rd, we may conjecture that it was an occasion for helping the sky-god to recover his powers of furnishing light, after the darkness of the winter solstice.

Juppiter, in early cult, was regularly grouped with two other gods, Mars and Quirinus. The former of these was certainly a war-god, but it is equally certain that war was not his only function. He was a high god, with a range of activities not common in the native Roman cult, whose usual principle seems to have been that one god should exercise one kind of *numen*, not many. What kind Mars began with no one can say at this date, especially as the problem is complicated by the ancients' habit of identifying him with the Greek Ares, who was nothing more than a war-god, a divine swashbuckler. But it is well attested that his cult was popular all over Italy, including Etruria, where he was adopted, like several other native Italian deities, and his name slightly altered into Maris. Various Italian dialects had also their own forms, and Latin itself varied somewhat, calling him on occasion Mavors, for instance, or by the re-duplicated name Marmar. He also has, not uncommonly, the title Gradivus, the meaning of which was already lost in classical antiquity. But that, whatever form his name took, he was not merely a god of battles is shown, among other evidence, by one of our oldest authorities, Cato the Censor (234-149 B.C.), in his curious little treatise on agriculture. He gives directions for a "vow for the health of the cattle", consisting partly in an offering of food and wine, to be made in the daytime, either by a freeman or a slave, and directed to Mars Silvanus. The recipient is distinctly a man's god, for no woman may be present nor see how the rite is performed, but there is no hint that he is warlike. He also prescribes a form of lustration for the fields, rather different from the Ambarvalia described by Tibullus (p. 35). The victims are a young boar-pig, a male lamb and a bull-calf ; Janus and Juppiter are associated with Mars in the ritual, a libation of wine being made to them at the beginning, but the prayer is addressed to Mars alone. It is quite long and explicit, and instead of praying, as one would expect if Mars was a god of war, that he would keep enemies of flesh and blood away from the fields, or give victory to Roman arms so that no invasion need be feared, the farmer asks him to ward off "diseases visible and invisible", bad weather, and other things which have little or nothing to do with war and its ravages, and to grant health to all who work on the farm. Nevertheless, his warlike functions are abundantly attested by his festivals and the nature of other deities associated with him, as will presently appear. We must therefore suppose that he was simply one of the great powers in which the Italian peoples trusted, their mighty protector and helper in both war and peace. The stormy history of early Rome is reason enough for Mars's warlike activities to have become strongly emphasised ; we shall see that on occasion not only he and other gods but so unlikely a power as Juno was thought to be capable of leading the State to battle, or defending it by force of arms.

The Roman year was ushered in by Mars' own month, which we still call, in the modern European languages, by various corruptions of the Latin name Martius. There was a festival in his honour, the details of which we do not know, on March 1st, although the Kalends are regularly Juno's day, and indeed there was a feast of married women, the Matronalia, at the same date. On the 14th—an unusual time for an official festival, since the rule is that only odd-numbered days of the month are employed for such purposes—came the Equirria, or horse-festival, the second of that name, for one had been held already at the close of the previous year, on February 27th. Both seem to have consisted in horse-races, held on the Field of Mars (Campus Martius), lying north of the older part of the City, unless the river was in flood, when they took place on the higher ground of the Caelian Hill, not far from the Forum. Horses were not used for agriculture, so it is clear that the object was to get the cavalry mounts ready for the coming campaigning season ; in early communities, fighting seldom or never took place in winter. Running, dancing and all forms of vigorous movement are well-known and common devices for increasing one's store of *mana*, and no doubt it was felt that the horses would be thus provided with needful *numen*, by the blessing of the god. Although the Ides of the month were not devoted to Mars, he was duly honoured on the first odd-numbered day thereafter, the 17th, when he had what is described as an *agonium*, a ritual word for a festival, again unknown in its details. The next lucky date, the 19th, known as the Quinquatrus, i.e., the fifth day (counting inclusively) after the Ides, was again sacred to him ; in the times when most of our authors wrote, two curious mistakes had altered the nature of this festival. It so happened that the temple of Minerva on the Aventine was dedicated on that day, and also the true meaning of the old-fashioned word had been forgotten, and it was imagined that it signified a festival lasting five days. Accordingly, for five days in the middle of Mars' month, the Romans from the second century B.C. onwards celebrated the intrusive goddess, her protégés, the craftsman of all kinds, including those who practiced the liberal arts, and not least schoolmasters, keeping holiday, while the last-named expected a fee from their pupils. Finally, on March 23rd, the festival of the Tubilustrium was held, that is to say the purification of the trumpets.

And here it may be well to state briefly what a Roman meant by the words *lustrum*, *lustrare*, and their compounds. To "lustrate" anything is to purify it, getting rid of evil or hostile influences and, if possible, getting good influences in. One of the commonest methods, although by no means the only one, was to draw the magic circle about the person or things needing purfication, as we have seen done at the Ambarvalia (p. 35) and Lupercalia. Examples of such rites are very common, and it was usual (the running at the Lupercalia was an exception) to move in a solemn and leisurely procession when performing the ceremony. Hence it is that the words often have the secondary meaning of orderly and impressive movement ; for Vergil, the clouds "lustrate" the mountain glens, that is, pass slowly over them, casting their shadows as they go. No doubt when a boy he had often seen them doing it on the higher ground towards the Alps, the *alto Mantovano* of to-day, which lies to the north of his native city of Mantua. But the ritual meaning was that of purification by whatever means, and hence a period of five years was called a *lustrum*, for then, by old custom, the censors, who used to be regularly appointed at that interval, would assemble the people, perform an appropriate ceremony, and so "put the *lustrum* away" (*lustrum condere*), probably by burying the materials they had used, with all the ill-luck or ill-doing of the period just closed sticking to them.

But to return to Mars, during March another important piece of war-magic took place, nothing less than a war-dance by his own priests. These were called simply the Dancers or Leapers, *Salii*, and their whole performance showed their antiquity. There were twenty-four of them altogether, the Salii Palatini and the Salii Collini, associated respectively with the primitive settlement on the Palatine and what appears to have been a later one on the Quirinal Hill (*Collis Quirinalis*). They all wore bronze armour and cloaks called *trabeae*, embroidered in bright colours, red and purple. They carried shields shaped somewhat like a figure 8 on their left arms, and a spear or stick in the right hand. On their heads they wore the same mitre-like covering as the flamens (p. 61), the *apex*. Thus attired, they passed through the city to several sacred places in it, dancing and leaping vigorously, beating their shields, and singing a very ancient hymn in honour, not only of Mars, but of a variety of gods, the surviving fragments of which (for its archaic text was often quoted by grammarians) still puzzle modern linguists. This obviously was primarily a war-dance, and the impression is not lessened by the fact that certain girls, the *Saliae uirgines* or dancing maidens, were somehow associated with them, for it is not very uncommon to find the woman of the tribe assisting their men in war-magic. But not the least interesting point is the form of their shields, which is known to be very ancient, appears with no great variety in sundry parts of the Mediterranean, and was associated by the Romans with a legend that the original model of them fell from heaven and the rest were made in close imitation of it, lest the sacred thing itself be stolen by some enterprising enemy. How important these representatives of an obsolete type of armour were is clear from the fact that the ancients commonly said, not that the Salii were performing or had ceased to perform their rites, but that the sacred shields (*ancilia ;* ordinary shields are *scuta* or *clipei*, according to their shape) were being moved, or were laid away.

For the next six months Mars had no regular worship (though of course a soldier in difficulties might pray to him as much as he saw fit, if it was done with decent observance of proper form) except for a second Tubilustrium which took place, we do not know why, on May 23rd. With October his ritual began again, for by then the summer and autumn work of the farm is over and the old campaigning-season likewise, so it was well to do two things, pass out of the condition into which the rites of March had brought the god's people, in other words dismiss the *numen* no longer needed, and procure new *numen* for the business lying ahead, the late autumn ploughing. The former purpose was achieved on October 19th, when the Armilustrium took place ; it must have seemed obvious that weapons which had been used against the enemy might be tainted with foreign magic or other undesirable forms of *numen*, for such things are as contagious as any disease, and therefore they should be purified before being laid away till next campaigning season. It may very well be, though we have no information, that if some disturbance did break out during the colder and darker time of year, some sort of observance was gone through by those who had to deal with it, but at least the "lustrated" equipment could do no harm in the meantime.

But a much more interesting ceremony, one which shows Mars in his double capacity as war-god and god of a farming community, took place on the Ides of the month, not displacing but together with the usual sacrifice to Juppiter on that day. This was the October Horse (*Ecus October*), and was conducted as follows. A horse-race was held, the contestants, as was usual in Rome, driving chariots, a vehicle which was never used, as far back as our records go, by Italians for actual war, though no doubt it once had been, but was retained for sport, as it was in Greece also. When it was over, the off horse of the winning team was sacrificed by the Flamen Martialis, Mars' own priest, who had restrictions and ceremonial comparable to those of the better-known Flamen Dialis, but less complicated and rigid. Its head and tail were cut off ; the former was taken by a runner to the Regia, for no doubt in older times the king was the only person fit to be trusted with such important magic, and there hung up over the hearth, on which its blood was allowed to drip. The head was fought for by the men of the Sacred Way and the Suburra, the winning party taking it away to its own quarter. To understand this properly, we must clear our minds of any preconceived notions about Mars. Very good scholars have been so blinded by the fact that a warlike beast is sacrificed to a god who certainly has warlike functions that they could see no further. But not only have we the distinct testimony, handed down it is true only in the epitome of an epitome, of Verrius Flaccus, the best antiquary of the age of Augustus, that the rite was performed to secure a good harvest, but we know that the head of the horse was garlanded with loaves of bread, and also that the blood was collected by the Vestals and kept in Vesta's own store-room, whence it was given out at the Parilia (see p. 74) as one of the materials for purifying the cattle-stalls. But all these facts must not make us conclude hastily, as some, including the present writer, have done, that the horse was one example the more of a vegetation-power in horse shape ; we have no evidence for this particular belief on Roman soil. It is a vigorous beast ; it is sacrificed to a great god ; all sacrifices produce *numen*, and this one not least. That war, tillage and stock-breeding should all be associated with the rite in one way or another does but prove that Mars was a great god, one of the few who no longer confine themselves to manifesting one kind of *numen*. Mars is also one of the very few deities who found themselves cramped, not enlarged, by identification with a Greek god. Once the notion became general that he was simply Ares under another name, his wider functions were so lost that it is only in quite recent times that any attention has been paid them.

Quirinus also suffered. He had his festival, the Quirinalia of February 17th, and his priest, the Flamen Quirinalis, who with his colleagues the priests of Juppiter and Mars made up the triad of greater flamens. But of the festival we know nothing, and of the priest, by an odd chance, only that he was active on occasion at functions with which so far as our evidence goes Quirinus was not connected. He had his place in the worship of Robigus, Larentia and Consus (pp. 73, 81 and 75), but we do not know how he served his own god. Nor is the deity in much better case. Ancient tradition had it that he was of Sabine origin, an odd fact, for the Sabine dialect lacked the sound expressed by *qu*. Setting this aside, it is pretty clear that the name is an adjective, and means "of the *quirium*", and that suggests Quirites, one of the words for citizens of Rome. A modern and very plausible etymology derives *quirium* from a supposed older form *couirium*, which would mean "assembly of men", and could quite easily become *quirium* in the mouths of Latin-speaking people. It may be, therefore, that he is the god who presides over the assembled citizens of his town, whether that was originally Rome or some place in the Sabine hills. Again Greek explanations have been the death of a Roman tradition ; he was associated with Mars, Mars was Ares, Ares had associated with him, or bore as a title, Enyalios, therefore Quirinus was Enyalios, a minor war-god. Furthermore, he was Romulus, the founder, in a thoroughly Greek story, of Rome, who, again in Greek and quite un-Roman fashion, had become a god after his death and was himself the son of Mars. But for the stolid Roman conservatism which went on performing traditional rites long after everyone had forgotten what they meant, we should be entirely in the dark concerning Quirinus.

Of Juno, on the other hand, we know a good deal, though her name has given rise to much debate among etymologists, some of whom affirm and some deny that it has any connexion with that of Juppiter. Two things at least are certain, that she is not associated with him in any early Roman worship and that she is closely connected with the life of women, like the Greek Hera, with whom she was identified. It has already been mentioned that she is capable of becoming a war-goddess (p. 63). This was at Lanuvium, perhaps also at Falerii and Tibur, but not at early Rome itself, so far as we know. In the first of these places she bore the titles Sispes and Sospita, both meaning Preserver, with the honourable additions Mater Regina, i.e., Mother (in the sense already explained, p. 22) and Queen. Her statue, whose age and origin we do not know, showed her, says Cicero,

> wearing a goat-skin, carrying a spear and buckler, and in shoes with upturned toes.

The skin had the horned head still on it, drawn over the head of the goddess, who thus appeared in a sort of primitive armour, ready to fight for her city if need arose. But these cults were somewhat abnormal, and generally she had quite other functions. In Roman worship she was never the chief deity, therefore had no need to fight, for that was the business of Mars, probably also of Quirinus, certainly of Juppiter, who was worshipped as Stator, i.e., Stayer of Rout, and one of whose festivals, the Poplifugia, may possibly mean the putting to flight of hostile armies, for that is what *populus*, the word from which English "people" is derived, really means. Her concern for women began, it would seem, with their birth and lasted all their lives. As Juno Lucina, she watched over the entry of the baby to the light (cf. p. 41) from the darkness of the womb. As Sororia, she cared for girls attaining maturity (*sororiare* is used of the swelling breasts of an adolescent girl). As goddess of marriage, she was Juno Iuga, Juno of the Yoke, if that was not a mere translation of the title Zygia, which has the same meaning and was borne by her Greek sister. Certainly the sanctity of marriage was in her charge, for an ancient law, attributed to the times of the kings, forbade a woman living in an irregular union with a married man to touch her altar, on pain of an expiatory sacrifice. Every year there was celebrated in her honour a rude and curious rite known as the Nonae Caprotinae, that is to say the Nones of the wild fig-tree. In the times of which we have any accurate knowledge, it was conducted by slave-girls ; it is very likely that in older days the free women of Rome performed it

themselves, but the classical Roman matron was of more than
Victorian correctness and dignity of manner. Its date was the
Nones (seventh) of Quintilis, the later July. Incidentally, it
is one of the indications that the festivals in the existing
calendar are older than the calendar itself, for this important
feast does not fall within the goddess's own month of June
(*Iunius*, derived, not directly from the Latin name of Juno,
but from its Etruscan mispronunciation Uni or rather a
compromise-form connected therewith ; *Iuno* could give only
Iunonius). Putting together the various accounts we have, and
subtracting the attempts at explanation of the ancients, who
manifestly had not the least idea what it was all about, we
learn that women both bond and free joined in a sacrifice
to Juno ; that they met and feasted under a wild fig-tree
and were crowned with its leaves ; that the slave-girls were
dressed in the full ceremonial costume of free women ; and
that they had a sham-fight with each other, apparently armed
with switches of fig-wood. To a modern's broader knowledge
of the early history of religion all is fairly clear. These slave-
girls acted as the substitutes of their mistresses, whose
clothing they wore, for that part of the rite which, as already
said, was below the ladies' dignity in historical times. They
used, in their contest, in other words in a rite of mutual
beating, rods from that tree which is employed to fertilise
the cultivated fig ; for the latter is female, and only the wild
fig, which is male, has the pollen which the cultivated fruits
must have to reach maturity. They thus knocked fertility
into each other, much as the Luperci (p. 58) struck it into
any whom they met with their similar magical implements ;
for in Latin a wild fig is a goat-fig (*caprificus*), and like names
produce like effects in all magical rites. Juno thus is once
more associated with at least the efficacious name of the
creature whose hide we saw her wearing.

Juno had a further development, which she shares with
several deities connected with the life and functions of women.
The sexual rhythm of their bodies tends to fall into periods
about equal in length to a lunar month, and this tendency
was strongly recognized by the Romans, for instance in their
computation of the full time of a normal pregnancy, ten lunar

months. Hence the goddess took on a secondary association with the moon. By ancient usage, the junior member of the College of Pontiffs (see p. 80) used to watch for the new moon, and would thereupon announce the length of the month just beginning by pronouncing, in presence of the assembled people and certain others of the State clergy, the formula *calo Iuno Couella*, "Juno Covella, I call", five or seven times according as the Nones were to be the fifth or the seventh, and the Ides consequently the thirteenth or the fifteenth. What the epithet Covella means we do not know, however.

Other developments of her cult are more obscure in their origins. For example, we do not know why she was worshipped on the Arx, the ancient citadel of Rome, on the Capitoline Mountain, at the end away from the Capitol proper, where the great temple (p. 59) stood, under the title Moneta, "the adviser or warner".

Something has already been said of the cult of Tellus Mater, the earth-goddess, at the Fordicidia (p. 18). She was conjoined to Ceres, the corn-goddess, in an ancient rite never quite confined to a fixed date, though it was always in January, on two days a week apart, the *feriae sementiuae*, or festival of the sowing, whose import is explained clearly and correctly by Ovid, as occurring "when the seed is cast and the field becomes fertile", i.e., at the end of the sowing of the winter wheat which is the main crop. Ceres, it would appear, was worshipped on the former of the two days and given an offering of spelt, Tellus on the second, her sacrifice being a sow in farrow. Ceres had once a male partner, Cerus, of whom nothing more is known than his name; foreign influence, especially Greek, gave her new associations and also functions which it is doubtful if she originally possessed. Roman gods of the oldest stratum were worshipped within the *pomerium* of the City, and this did not include the Aventine Hill, although that lay within the city limits, or what we should regard as such; the inhabited region so outgrew its old sacral boundaries that a magistrate going from one part of Rome to another might find himself obliged to perform the rites of divination proper to one quitting his own territory and moving across the border. The Aventine, being close at hand and a convenient site, became a favourite spot for the temples of deities whose existence was recognized by the Roman government, though they were not on the same footing as the original objects of worship. One of these was Ceres in a new guise, associated with Liber and Libera, the former an Italian god of wine and the latter his female partner or double ; Italian deities not infrequently go in pairs of male and female, though they were not thought of as married, so that whichever sex it pleases them to have, appropriate formulae may be addressed to them. But the group would seem to go back by some route to the great cult of Demeter at Eleusis, where she was associated with her daughter Kore and a god Iakchos. A similarity of name caused Iakchos to be confused with Bakchos, in other words Dionysos, who included an interest in viticulture among his many activities, and so Liber, also identified with Dionysos, represented Iakchos at Rome. It is, then, a Greek cult in Italian dress, and the temple became a centre, not only for the corn-dealers who apparently had much to do with its introduction, but for the religious and other activities of the *plebs*, that part of the population which, not being able to show descent from original inhabitants of Rome or early accretions to their number, had to begin with no share either in the State cult or in its secular offices, though during the Republic they attained to both in full measure. Parallel to this political change came a change in religion, to the extent of giving real importance to several divinities who had not originally been worshipped in Rome at all, and whose festivals therefore were never added to those recorded in large letters on the calendars. But of these accessions more will be said in the next chapter. For the present, it is enough to notice that the Aventine temple was founded on Ceres' own feast-day, the Cerialia of April 19th, when again she was associated with Tellus, for that date is the next odd-numbered day but one after the Fordicidia. Another effect, it may be, of foreign, perhaps specifically Greek influence was that Ceres was regarded at times as formidable, for a mad person was thought to be possessed either by the Larvae, or ghosts, apparently much the same as the Lemures (p. 33), or else by her, and was called accordingly *laruatus* or *cerritus*. Demeter has her formidable side, for the dead are sometimes called her people and one of her titles is Erinys, or Avenging Power. This may have influenced Ceres, who naturally was identified with her, as both were corn-deities.

Other agricultural rites also were maintained, not merely permitted or regulated, by the State, and not the least remarkable was the Robigalia. It took place on April 25th, and Ovid claims to have seen the ritual ; whether this is true or he merely read a good account of it matters little.

"As I was on my way back from Nomentum," he says, "on this day, I was stopped on the road by a congregation all in white. It was a *flamen* on his way to the sacred grove of ancient Rust (*robigo*), to burn the sacrificial portions of a dog and of a sheep. I at once drew near to learn the ceremony, and Quirinus' own priest spoke thus". (He then gives the substance of the prayer, a long appeal to Rust not to damage the crops.) "Such were his words. At his right hand were a napkin loosely woven, also a chalice of wine and a box of incense. Incense he put and wine he poured into the altar-fire, also the flesh of the sheep and the hideous entrails—I saw him do it—of the dog".

Other authorities inform us that the name of the power addressed was Robigus, *robigo* being the ordinary word for the "rust" which on occasion damages wheat, and that the grove was five miles from Rome, which would bring it about to the boundary of the oldest Roman territory. Clearly the intention is to check the incursions of the disease within the limits of all Roman fields, just at that time of year when it is most likely to occur, and all manner of farming activities were introduced by the sacrifice of a dog or puppy, presumably to the powers beneath the earth, which were often supposed to be pleased with that offering ; but why the *flamen* of Quirinus in particular was employed in it is a matter for conjecture, and no explanation yet put forward has satisfied everyone.

Flora was the goddess, not so much of flowers in general, as of the flowering of the wheat and other crops. Her festival apparently depended on her coming, that is to say on the

time when the flowering occurred, for it never was fixed in
the calendar until it had quite lost its original character. The
Floralia of approximately the end of April were buried under
the Floral Games (*Ludi Florales*) of April 28th-May 3rd,
which in turn grew out of the one-day celebration of the
erection of a temple to her on the first of these dates. It was
ordered by a Sibylline oracle (cf. p. 95), which meant that
it was a Greek cult, and the loose nature of the festival, the
central feature of which was farces of a not over-decent kind
acted by courtesans (in ancient "legitimate drama", female
parts were taken by men), suggests that it was an offshoot
of one of the semi-Oriental cults which lurked here and
there under the worship of Aphrodite, one of whose titles
was Antheia, She of the Flowers. That temple was at the
Circus Maximus, in the valley between the Palatine and
Aventine, unromantically occupied in recent years by a gas-
works ; the old Flora had her inconspicuous shrine on the
Quirinal, and it was a custom to bring stalks of corn to it on
the day called Florifertum, whether that was the same as the
Floralia or not. Doubtless they were flowering, not ripe stalks.
We know even less of Pomona, goddess of tree-fruits, but
she must once have had a certain importance, for she is one
of the fifteen deities who had special priests (*flamines*) of their
own, though hers is the most junior of all.

We are rather better acquainted with the Pales, a god and
a goddess, so old a pair that the surviving authors had quite
forgotten that they were a pair at all and use the name in the
singular, making it masculine or feminine as the humour
takes them ; a single entry in the Fasti Antiates (p. 52) lets
us know that on the Nones of Quintilis (July 7th) there was
some kind of festival to "the two Pales". A better known
occasion, however, was April 21st, the Parilia (etymologically,
this should be Palilia, since it means "feast of the Pales",
but such differentiation, as it is called, is very common in
many tongues). The Pales were deities of stock-breeding and
all that goes with it ; and that a festival of the kind to be
described should have taken place at a comparatively late
time in the year, when the Italian spring is well advanced,
suggests that it had its origin with some element in the

Roman population whose old home was much further north. Certainly it resembles a formal preparation of the beasts for leaving their winter quarters and venturing out to graze and live in the open.

The procedure was as follows. Every owner of stock was provided by the Vestals with the necessary materials for purification, the blood of the October horse, the ashes of the unborn calf of the Fordicidia, and bean-husks. The first two obviously can have been given but in minute quantity to each person, of the last there would be abundance. With these he fumigated his byres at dawn, having first sprinkled the beasts with water and swept the stalls clean. Various other forms of fumigation were in use at all events in the time of Ovid, but the most conspicuous, which was applied to the people concerned, perhaps to the beasts also, was to jump through the flames of a bonfire of light materials, straw and the like. There was the usual garlanding of everything and everyone concerned, and rustic sports. The sacrifice seems to have included no animal victims ; a prayer for divine protection (whereof Ovid gives us what purports to be a paraphrase, at best an extremely free one) was repeated, with the face to the east, four times. This was the individual method of keeping the day ; there was also State ritual, but we know no details of it. Nor is it clear how the idea started that the day was the anniversary of the City's foundation, a notion popular throughout a great part of antiquity and revived by the late Fascist government of Italy.

Another pair of rustic deities were Consus and Ops, that is to say Storer and Plenty. Omitting much Greek lore which conceals their real natures, for these ancient figures puzzled the later people of antiquity, we know the following facts about them. Consus had an underground altar in the Circus Maximus (cf. p. 74), which was uncovered only on his festivals. Its character may perhaps be connected, as has been suggested, with the common practice of storing corn in underground receptacles, but if so, it certainly never was such a store-bin itself nor near one, for that low-lying ground would be under water, or at least waterlogged, when the Tiber was in flood in the earlier and less well-drained ages of Rome.

A fragment of old lore concerning the god has come down to us, preserved because by some blunder it was not only wrongly understood but imagined to be the inscription on the altar itself, which is quite impossible. It runs, when properly interpreted, "Consus is mighty in the sowing, Mars in war, the Lares at the boundary between farms", thus combining in one dictum two purely rustic powers with the great god whose scope included the protection of the land and those who worked on it. That Consus's activities should extend to sowing is perfectly understandable, for if there were no bins to store corn in, where should we get the seed to sow ? It is the business of the power whose *numen* helps men to store away corn or any other useful thing also to help them get it out when they want it, and gods, both Roman and other, very commonly have functions which seem opposed, being complementary opposites. It has been the fashion of late in some places to speak of "bi-polar" activities in such a connexion. The festivals of the god and his companion were in August and December. In the former month, the Consualia came on the 21st, the Opiconsivia on the 25th. By that time, a Roman harvest is in ; the lower-lying parts of the country have generally cut their wheat by about July 31st at latest, though hilly districts may be a little later. It was therefore no inappropriate time for the deities who watched over the store-bins and their abundant contents to be celebrated. A little less obvious is the December date (Consualia December 15th, Opalia December 19th, with the Saturnalia intervening), for it corresponds to no very obvious part of the cycle of farm-work. One suggestion is that it marks the very last gathering of all, the collection of the latest olives, for these are not got in all at once, but in successive stages at not inconsiderable intervals of time. Certainly they too have to be stored, and a plentiful supply of them is welcome, and must always have been so.

The Saturnalia have been mentioned in passing ; it was the festival of a mysterious deity, Saturnus or Saeturnus (usually Saturn in English), of whom exceedingly little is really known, although many confident assertions have been made. Of one thing at least we may be fairly sure, that he is not originally Roman, for we have it on good authority that sacrifice was made to him with uncovered head. That is the ordinary Greek rite, presumably to let that important part of the sacrificer's person be open to the benign influence of the god he addressed, but a Roman cautiously muffled his head on such occasions, lest his efforts be nullified by hearing or seeing a bad omen ; for omens are of no effect and portend nothing if no one, or even if no official person, observes them. What the god's name means, we do not know. Attempts to find it a Latin etymology have so far proved fruitless, and at present it is generally supposed that it has something to do with the Etruscan family name Satre or Satria. In that case, he probably has no real name at all, but is simply "the god whom the *Satre* worship". But even this is far from certain, for our knowledge of how words borrowed from Etruscan, which in any case were not numerous, were treated, is far from complete. His chief festival, the Saturnalia, originally on December 17th, but later extended to three, four, five or even seven days, to begin with resembled the Greek harvest-feast of the Kronia[1], for during it there were no social distinctions, slaves had a holiday and feasted like their masters, and all restrictions were relaxed, one being the prohibition on gambling with dice, which was supposed to be in force at other times of the year. It was, however, a more thoroughgoing season of jollity than the Kronia, at least in historical times, "the best of all days," says Martial. Civilians and soldiers alike celebrated it, it was usual to choose by lot a Lord of Misrule (*Saturnalicius princeps*, "leading man of the Saturnalia"), and gifts were exchanged. Although the date is different, it seems probable that its customs, blending with those of the New Year festival and with the northern Yule, had their share in producing the traditional merry-makings of Christmas (cf. p. 148). However, there are indications that Saturn had a grim side to his character, for not only is he identified with Kronos, and through him with unlovely Semitic gods worshipped on occasion with human sacrifices, but his cult-partner is Lua Mater, whose name, if, as seems probable, it is Latin, is to

[1] See the author's *Ancient Greek Religion*, p. 67.

be connected with *lues*, "plague, pestilence, blight", while of her cult we know this much, that arms taken from the enemy were on occasion dedicated to her by burning them (clearly a piece of sympathetic magic, to spoil the arms the enemy still had), a rite which she shares with Mars and with his cult-partner Nerio, an obscure goddess made more obscure by her becoming identified with Minerva.

Agriculture, with which it has commonly been thought that Saturn was somehow connected, had a few other deities, mostly quite minor. Liber Pater, the wine-god, has been mentioned ; there are not a few obscurities connected with him. His name is identical with the word signifying "free", in the sense of free-born, not a slave, and on his feast-day, the Liberalia, March 17th, it was customary for young men to put on the man's toga (cf. p. 42) for the first time, on which occasion they were escorted to the Forum by their friends and relatives.   Liber is also a title of Juppiter, which may or may not be due to a translation into Latin of Zeus Eleutherios ; and naturally Liber became identified with Dionysos (cf. p. 72). The precise connexion between his various activities, and between him and Juppiter, cannot be said to have been clearly explained as yet. Another deity of wine was Medetrina, a goddess whose existence seems due to the festival called Medetrinalia, on October 11th, when it was the custom formally to taste the product of the recent vintage, not yet properly fermented into wine, with the formula "I drink new and old wine, I heal (*medeor*) my illness, new and old". In passing, a minor deity of the fields should be mentioned, because her name has been much misinterpreted in ancient and modern times. This is Mater Matuta, who had a festival, the Matralia, on June 11th, and a temple in the Cattle-Market. A perfectly satisfactory explanation of her name has come down to us, and is due to Varro ; she looked after the ripening (*maturescentia*) grains. This fits the time of her festival, not very long before harvest, also the fact that her feast was in the hands of free married women, for clearly her share in the provision of *numen* for the fields was important enough to demand the attention of these traditional practitioners of farm-magic and doers of the lighter farm work. It equally explains why no slave-woman might take part ; slaves are foreigners, and what should they know of the way to approach the native goddess ? Equally, it makes it clear why some Greek theologians thought she was the same person as their own Eileithyia, the goddess of birth ; if she can ripen the fruit of the ground, why not that of the womb, seeing that the equation between Mother Earth and human mothers runs through all ancient religion and magic ? But the same root which gives Latin its word for "ripen" produces several words which signify "early", especially early in the day. So the notion came about and is not yet quite departed that she was a dawn-goddess. It is refuted by the fact that she had a cult. Dawn—Eos in Greek, Aurora in Latin—is a pretty figure of mythology and folk-tales, whom no one is known to have worshipped in the whole ancient world.

Water had of course its deities, the best-known of whom is Neptunus (usually curtailed to Neptune in English), a not very important god of fresh water, who never became a god of the sea (the Romans were and remained incurable land-lubbers, though necessity compelled them to voyage for trade and to maintain a navy) until he came into contact with the Greek Poseidon, which explains why he was sacrificed to at sea with Greek and not Roman ritual. His feast, the Neptunalia, was on July 23rd, a very natural time to appeal to a power who could give water, in the heat of an Italian summer when streams were low and fires likely to break out among the houses. His cult-partners were Salacia, apparently the goddess who makes water spring up (*salire*) from the ground, and Venilia, about whom nothing more is known. More important, in Rome at least, was the god of the Tiber, though he does not seem to have borne in ritual the name of his river ; it has been guessed that Volturnus, a god of probably Etruscan connexions, who had a *flamen* of his own, was the Tiber-god, but this is simply a guess, and its author, Mommsen, backed it up by some very bad etymology. Whatever the deity was officially called, he had some interesting ritual which gave rise to a whole class of Roman priests, the *pontifices* or bridge-builders, whose name is commonly Anglicised into "pontiffs". Their original business must have been to appease the river when it was necessary to throw a bridge over it, thus putting it and its god in the magically inferior position of being under the feet of those who walked across. A little of their magic we know, for it survives in a very old rite, much discussed and misunderstood in antiquity and by moderns, that of the Argei. This word (its etymology is uncertain) signified certain dummies of straw, in an old-fashioned costume, and also the chapels, twenty-seven in number, in each of which one such figure was kept till needed. On May 14th, an even-numbered day and therefore a strange and unusual one for any public ceremony, for the Romans believed firmly in the luck of odd numbers, these puppets were taken to the old wooden bridge, the Pons Sublicius, which spanned the river, and there, in the presence of the pontiffs and the Vestals, were solemnly thrown in. The only reasonable explanation, as demonstrated by the late Sir J. G. Frazer, is that they were surrogates for human beings, and the river was expected to accept them instead of drowning real men who used the bridge. Why the number was twenty-seven and not some other we cannot tell; it may be related to some ancient subdivision of either the City or the ground on which it stands.

Other deities of water included Fons, a sort of collective god of all fountains or springs (*fontes*), and a few more, mostly obscure and sometime doubtful, while numerous minor godlings presided each over some one stream or spring. For all sources of water, especially of drinkable water, are holy in most countries, and not least around the Mediterranean, where a good water-supply, such as Imperial Rome acquired and the modern city has regained, is not always easy to come by, especially in summer.

Fire had, besides Vesta, its gods and goddesses, two of whom, Cacus and Caca, were perhaps those presiding over the fire of the chief's hut in the old Palatine settlement; at all events we know that Caca had a ceremonial like that of Vesta, and the position of the latter's shrine in the Forum, not a part of the oldest Rome, is one of several indications that she was not the oldest sacred hearth. A very different god was Volcanus (Vulcan in English), whose name is certainly not Latin, for its nearest connexions seem to be with Crete and Etruria, and whose original functions were connected with the volcanic phenomena which we name after him. He too had a festival in hot weather, when his destructive fires were most to be feared, on August 23rd, when he was given a sacrifice likely to please a fire-god, live fish being thrown into flames. Thus getting the sort of victim whose habitat would generally protect it effectively against him, he might be the readier to spare land-dwellers, their crops, houses and cattle. Inevitably, in time he was equated with Hephaistos, the Greek smith-god, who had himself begun as a deity of volcanic regions, and so passes out of native Roman religion into the cult and mythology of the all-pervading Greeks. His partner Maia was still more effectively hidden, for, her name happening to sound like that of Maia the daughter of Atlas, mother of Hermes in Greek legend, her original nature was almost completely forgotten.

The gods of the underworld received their dues at Roman hands, but with cautious reserve, for no one wanted to come into too close contact with such powers while in this life. The State did not directly concern itself with the placation of ghosts, whether members of Roman families or kinless and homeless phantoms, but it set aside days on which they might be dealt with according to custom by individual households. The Lemuria of May have been mentioned (p. 33), also the soul-feast of February (p. 48), the *dies parentales*, or days for *parentalia*, such rites as are due to a departed father or mother, and so to dead kin generally. But there were a few deities who seem to belong to the same sphere. It is said by sundry ancients that *parentalia* were given to two women of old days, Tarpeia and Acca Larentia, or Larentina, for the name varies a little. It needs no great research into the facts to see that they are minor goddesses, whose activities were somehow connected with the underworld, but whether or not they were actually rulers over the dead we do not know enough to say. Evidently their ceremonial was like enough to that conducted at a grave to point to their being other than the familiar and friendly givers of *numen* to the crops. Dim and unsatisfactory memories exist also of a deity called Vediovis, that is to say "not Juppiter", who was important enough to have two temples dedicated to him in Republican times. It possibly is he whom Dionysios of Halikarnassos means when he says that if a client wronged his patron or a patron his client

"he was liable under the law of treason which Romulus sanctioned, and if found guilty might be killed by anyone who chose to do so, as being a victim to Zeus of the underworld"

But it is perhaps more likely that Dionysios is merely giving Greek definiteness to the grim Roman formula concerning such an offender, *sacer esto*, let him be removed from ordinary life and relations ; the word *sacer*, which is very like the Polynesian term "tapu", has a double meaning. A *res sacra* is a piece of property of some kind made over to a god, and therefore, as we should call it, holy or sacred ; but a *homo sacer*, a man thus severed from the uses of everyday life, is rather a person accursed, left for the gods concerned, or some particular god, to deal with as may seem fit to divine wisdom.

But generally, the lower world was thought of as the home of the Manes, or Di manes, the "good folk" or "good gods". The usual form of inscription on a tombstone stated that it was dedicated to the *di manes*, and this was particularised by adding the name of the deceased, either in the dative ("to the Good Gods and especially to So-and-So") or in the genitive ("to the Good Gods of such a-one"). A name which not infrequently meets the student is, however, that of Orcus. It is a disputed point whether this is Latin at all ; there is a Greek underworld figure, Horkos, "the Oath", presumably that power who punishes perjurers, in this life or the next, and the Greek *h*, never a strong aspirate, tended to disappear and may well have been lost altogether in the passing of the name from one language to another ; Latin derivations, however, are not entirely given up, and it may be proved that Orcus is really a native god, possibly a sort of a Roman

Hades or Pluton. Pluton himself was, in the period of strong Greek influence, adopted by Roman theologians and mythologists, if not actually in cult, his name being either Latinised by dropping the final *n*, or translated as Dis Pater, "the wealthy one who has authority".

In so short an account as this many Roman deities known to be old must be omitted, especially as nothing is known of the functions of some of them. But mention may be made of one curious little goddess whose name seems to spring from a ritual formula. On the Ides of March, that is the first day of full moon in the year, it was customary to pray that one might live in and through the year (*annare perennareque*) in comfort. From the stems of these two verbs a name, Anna Perenna, seems to have grown up, and to her the festival of that day was dedicated. It was a popular ceremonial, involving a picnic in the open or under temporary shelters, on the banks of the Tiber, during which everyone drank as much as he could, for he hoped to live as many more years as he could drink cups of wine ; Ovid remarks drily that some assured themselves of a very long life indeed by this means. Anna, who was a real enough goddess to have a sacred grove in Rome, fell a prey to mythologists, owing to the fact that her name sounded rather like the Semitic Hannah, and Dido, queen of Carthage, was provided with a sister of that name in a story immortalised by Vergil.

The worship by the State of these deities was highly organised. At the head of the Roman clergy stood the Board of Pontiffs (*collegium pontificum*), which included, besides the Pontiffs themselves, who originally numbered three, but were successively increased to six, nine, fifteen and sixteen, the Flamines, of whom, besides the greater ones serving Juppiter, Mars and Quirinus, there were twelve more, some so obscure to us that we do not know to what deities they were assigned, the Vestal Virgins, and the King of the sacred rites (*Rex sacrorum*), the inheritor of the priestly functions of the real kings. Save for the chief pontiff (*pontifex maximus*), who was the head of the State clergy, he outranked all his colleagues. He was the only priest who must be that and nothing else ; presumably it was felt to be neither logical nor perhaps politic for one who was a king, even if only in name, to be also a republican magistrate. The greater flamens seldom held any secular office, owing to the onerous nature of their duties ; but there never was a priestly class or caste, nor was the clergy ever in a position to enforce any decisions it might make, even in purely religious matters. Its function was to advise, the advice being tendered to the executive officers of the State, who, if they accepted it, would see that it was carried out. It also guided the actual performance of any rites which might be decided upon, or which were regularly performed as a matter of course. In time a very large sacral literature was accumulated, but it dealt with ritual, not with doctrine, for the sufficient reason that Roman religion, like that of most ancient peoples, had no doctrine and nothing which could be called a creed. It was universally assumed that there were deities, and that they possessed *numen*, which might be used for the practical benefit of mankind. It was the business of the experts to discover and teach how best to induce the gods to do as men wished, also to ascertain whether they were willing to do so, or approved the actions begun or contemplated by their worshippers. To achieve this, it was proper to know the right names and epithets by which to address the powers in question, for a prayer cannot be addressed to no one. It was also essential to know the proper ritual, and often highly advisable to keep it secret, lest enemies should learn of it and use it against Rome instead of for her. If any god or goddess was known to favour a foreign power, it was lawful and prudent to induce him or her to desert, and for that purpose there existed a rite of "calling out" (*euocatio*) by which such deities might be drawn from their former abodes and brought to Roman territory, under promise of a better cult there than they had had before. It was in this way that Minerva was got from Falerii after its capture by the Romans in 241 B.C., and given a shrine on the Caelian Hill in Rome. In like manner, Juno Regina owed her temple on the Aventine to her quitting Veii when Camillus captured it ; the temple was dedicated in 392 B.C. It is clear that in all this there was an element of sheer magic ; there was also a strong element of bargaining, for the Romans

were a legal-minded people who understood excellently the
obligations of both parties to a contract. So on occasion they
made contracts with gods, drawn up by skilled clerical
draughtsmen and providing for all manner of contingencies.
A very famous one has come down to us. When it became
evident that the Second Punic War was to be a long and
hard-fought struggle, with Hannibal in Italy and threatening
Rome itself, Juppiter was appealed to and promised a sacrifice
of the whole increase of the flocks and herds for a year if by
that year, half a decade ahead, he put the Roman people in
a satisfactory position. The deed, when drawn up, was
approved by the Assembly. But in return for so great a gift,
the god was to waive certain rights which he might normally
insist on ; the Romans were to be considered to have done
their part even if irregularities were found in the method of
sacrificing, if the offering were made on the wrong date or
by an unqualified person, and also to be quit of responsibility
for any beasts who might die or be stolen before the time
came to offer them.

A further business of the clergy was to discover the will
of the gods, to the extent at least of knowing whether they
answered "yes" or "no" to a proposal made to them, as for
instance, to give their blessing to some public act about to
be commenced. Here lay the functions of the Augurs, literally
the Increasers (by magical or other supernatural means),
whose office had already shifted its emphasis by the time
we first learn anything about them from any process of
"increasing" anything to the more passive observance of the
signs by which the divine will was made known. The usual
process was as follows. The diviner began by tracing out a
limited region within which he would look for signs, a
templum, as it was technically called. This he did by in-
dicating visible landmarks, as (the example is from Varro),
"yonder tree, whatever kind it is, which I know I have
named, shall be the left-hand boundary of my *templum*"
and so forth. The space thus marked out was divided, as
by the *cardo* and *decumanus* of a land-surveyor (cf. p. 38),
into right and left, front and back ; signs within it had their
understood significance, according as they appeared in one

or another of these quarters. Since the diviner regularly faced south, left-hand omens were generally lucky, being from the east, the quarter of sunrise and so associated with light and all that it stands for. The usual signs were derived from the flight and cries of birds, hence the name for the taking of omens is *auspicium*, literally bird-watching, and anyone who had the official right and duty of looking for such signs in preparation for a piece of public business was said to have *auspicia*. A subordinate, for instance a junior officer on service, was governed by the *auspicia* of his senior, on whom devolved the responsibility for the subordinate's action and the official credit for any success. As in other priestly business, the augurs themselves were simply the expert advisers, whose part was to see that the watching for omens was properly done, or to do it themselves if so instructed by the legal authority. In later times the whole business degenerated into a mere farce. An action having been determined upon for secular reasons, good omens would be officially announced, even if none or only bad ones had actually been observed ; the responsibility rested on the person announcing them, and the gods, if they had not meant to approve the action, had their legal remedy in punishing that person. On the other hand, if it was desired to impede any public business, it was open to a magistrate who disapproved of it to announce bad omens and so bring it to a stop, or even to proclaim that he was going to "observe from the sky", as the technical phrase had it, and so suspend action until he had made his report. Some late Republican legislation was intended to stop this wresting of what had been a serious religious observance into a tool of political trickery.

Besides these great priestly *collegia*, or boards, and the later officials with whom the next chapter will deal, there were numerous minor bodies. One of the best known to us was the Arval Brothers *(Fratres aruales)*, a very old priesthood, revived by Augustus, whose records were carved on stone in the precinct of their goddess, the Dea Dia, and have been largely preserved. Their chief business was a series of complicated ceremonies carried out every year,

having for their object to secure *numen* for the crops. Of
the Salii and Luperci we have already spoken (pp. 65 and
57). But on all alike fell the task of seeing that everything
connected with the State religion, whether a sacrifice, the
dedication of a temple or altar, the taking of *auspicia* or
anything else was done according to the traditional methods,
known by long experience to be agreeable to the supernatural
powers, and that any failure in ritual was put right by an
expiatory sacrifice or other proper means. To observe all
these rites most scrupulously was the characteristic expression
of love and duty (*pietas*) towards the gods. Such observance
("care and ceremonies", Cicero calls it) was binding on all
right-thinking Romans. To bind is *religare*, and the feeling
of uneasiness if anything in this sphere was not properly
performed was therefore *religio*. All the sacred precautions
could be summed up by styling them the *religiones* of the
Roman people, perhaps the nearest equivalent in Latin to
speaking of their religion. The result of performing them in
the absolutely correct manner which ritual prescribed was
the maintaining of peaceful relations with the deities, comparable to the peaceful relations between one State and
another when both sides scrupulously observe the terms of
a treaty concluded between them. Hence a Roman spoke of
the "peace with the gods", *pax deorum*, and strove, prompted
by his *pietas*, to secure it.

It was thus not a very exalted religion. Its objects were
material, a sufficient food-supply, protection against physical
dangers such as fire, success in war, increase by natural means
of the population and their cattle. Nevertheless it was decent,
marked by no immoral rites and encumbered by no frivolous
or savage myths concerning gods and men. It seems to have
been felt that the gods did not make wanton use of their
numen, but dealt honestly and intelligibly with men who were
honest with them ; that they were possessed of that *grauitas*,
the disposition to take things seriously, which a Roman
admired in his fellows. The very vagueness of the conceptions
left a mystic or saint, if early Rome bred any, free to read
what exalted ideas he would into the traditional cults, un-
encumbered by either dogma (of which Greek religion was

equally free) or mythology. Left to itself, the old religion of Rome might in time have risen into something lofty and pure ; but we shall see that it was not left to itself, and what good qualities it might have developed were so buried under foreign accretions that it is only in the last two or three generations that we have formed any clear conception of what it was.

CHAPTER III

STRANGE GODS

It was not to be expected that a small state like early Rome, lying in the middle of Italy and on the great natural trade route, the Tiber valley, should long be left undisturbed, in religion or anything else, by the powerful influences about her. Immediately to the south were the territories of the Latin League, of which, from the earliest known times, Rome seems to have been a member, rising to be its head in place of the older state of Alba Longa, of which it is reputed that Rome itself was originally a colony. To the north lay the Etruscan confederation, a loose union of cities whose ruling class and some part at least of their population came originally from Asia. They had a high civilisation, a splendid architecture, a language differing entirely from any other in Europe and still unintelligible to us, a developed industry, an art greatly influenced by Greek models yet with original features, and a religion which, while it borrowed freely from Greek and Italian cults, had characteristics of its own, notably its extremely elaborate divination and the ceremonies with which its expert practitioners sought not only to foretell the future but also to delay the coming of an unwelcome event. Equally characteristic was the rich, complex and fantastic picture which they had formed of the other world and the experiences of the soul after death. These are portrayed on the walls of the elaborate tombs of their nobles and have a flavour at

times of the heavens and hells of far Eastern religions, mixed
with such familiar conceptions as the banquets and sports
of the blessed in something like a coarsened Greek Elysion ;
all very different from the shadowy Manes of Roman cult.
These people established a dynasty in Rome, the fall of which
led to the foundation of the Republic, and their contributions
to the religion of the City they ruled for a time, while not
affecting its fundamentals, were not inconsiderable. With
more or less probability, at times with something like certainty,
we may trace the following elements of Roman cult to the
Etruscans ; the dress and insignia of the magistrates, all of
whom had priestly functions, the style and orientation of the
older temples (*aedes sacrae*), the *templum* itself, although that
has been credited, not without plausibility, to the Bronze
Age inhabitants of pre-Etruscan Italy, the use of cult-statues
in worship, the elaborate funerals of nobles, and something
at least of the methods of divination. These last, however,
were not fully Etruscanized. The Etruscan experts, as already
said, claimed to foretell the future ; a Roman augur hardly
did more than learn whether or not the gods approved what
was actually begun or purposed, whether or not an offering
was acceptable to them. For further details, and especially
for an interpretation of any happening supposed to be preter-
natural and therefore ominous, official Rome resorted to what
were rudely called the "gut-gazers" (*haruspices*) of Etruria,
who never formed part of the Roman clergy but were sum-
moned from time to time to give their opinion. Not all
Romans believed in them, for at least the elder Cato remarked
that he wondered they could see each other without laughing,
but the skeptics were in the minority. Their characteristic
method, as their nickname implies, was to sacrifice a beast
and examine its entrails, especially the liver ; there survives
a bronze model of the liver of a sheep inscribed with names
of gods in Etruscan characters, and we know something, from
Latin references to works by Etruscans on the subject, of the
methods used. They were curiously like those employed by
the Dyaks at the present time, as may be seen at length in
the great work of Hose and McDougall, *The Pagan Tribes
of Borneo*. We have seen that Saturn may be an Etruscan

god, and several other deities have with more or less likelihood
been traced to the same people. On the whole, however,
Etruscan influence upon Rome was superficial, touching
several externals of the native religion but leaving its fundamental character, so far as we can judge, unaltered.

Naturally, other Italian communities of a culture very
like that of Rome itself and of about the same development
could effect no profound change in its religious life. They
did, nevertheless, give the Romans several new deities, whose
shrines, while not admitted to the charmed circle of the
pomerium, stood within the boundaries of the City, on such
places as the Aventine. Their adoption was due to various
causes. Diana, a goddess of forests who helped women by
giving them children, was the chief deity of the Latin League.
Her shrine was in a sacred grove, *nemus*, not far from Aricia ;
its site was near the modern village of Nemi. Rome, apparently while still under the Etruscan kings, had ambitions to
become the head of the League, and in connexion, it would
appear, with these set up a new and comparatively imposing
cult of the goddess on the Aventine, where some few features
of the temple and its attendant ceremonies still bore witness
in historical times of her native character, before she was
hidden under the personality of the Greek Artemis, whom
she really did resemble to a certain extent. Minerva has
already been mentioned as one of the triad worshipped in
the Capitoline Temple (p. 59) ; there is no evidence that
she had any cult in Rome earlier than that, but afterwards
she possessed several and took an important place, although
just outside the closed circle of the oldest deities, as patroness
of all manner of handicrafts and, later, of fine arts. An interesting importation was Fortuna, otherwise Fors Fortuna.
There are some fairly definite indications that she was
originally an agricultural deity, and a little evidence that she
had some connexion with Mater Matuta (cf. p. 78). In time,
however, perhaps because so much in agriculture depends
on causes outside the farmer's control, she became, like the
Greek Tyche, a goddess of luck or chance, and as such was
worshipped in many parts of Rome, and also elsewhere, under
a variety of titles, such as Fortune of the Men, of the Women,

of Maidens, and so forth. That she was not of the oldest Roman group of deities is clear from her having no festival, also from the story that she was introduced by King Servius Tullius, the last monarch but one of the traditional list, which is to all intents and purposes the same as saying that her cult, while old, is not of the most ancient. She may have come in from Antium (Anzio), where she was multiplied into two Fortunes, or from Praeneste (Palestrina), where she had a very famous oracle ; Antium also possessed such a shrine, but we know little about it. If so, however, she must have lost some of her powers on the way, for in Rome she was not oracular.

A few gods originally Greek seem to have reached Rome by way of Italian cities. Two of the most noteworthy are the divine twins, Kastor and Polydeukes, sons of Zeus and Leda, or, as they are called in Latin, Castor and Pollux, colloquially "the Castors". A picturesque tale, modelled on existing Greek legends, stated that at the battle of Lake Regillus, 499 B.C., they had appeared at the head of the Roman army and afterwards brought news to the City of its victory over the Latins. The facts about them are that they, particularly Castor, who overshadows his brother, were patrons of the Roman cavalry, the *equites*, and of the class from which it was drawn, originally young men of good families. The nearest place from which the twins could have been brought to Rome is Tusculum (Frascati), where they were worshipped from quite early times. A very interesting fact, attesting their early arrival in Rome, is that their temple stands (for the extensive ruins are still visible) inside the *pomerium*, in the Forum itself, near the shrine of Vesta.

Within a still older *pomerium*, however, is another Greek importation, Hercules, whose name is one of several Italian corruptions of Herakles. The ancient line followed by the Luperci (p. 57) swings away from the base of the Palatine at one place, for, as Tacitus puts it,

The furrow which traced the boundaries of the town began at the Cattle Market . . . to take in the great altar of Hercules.

The Cattle Market (*Forum boarium*) is on the side towards

the river, a natural place for traders coming up or down stream to meet the early inhabitants of Rome and exchange their wares for such things as living cattle or their meat, tallow and hides. But for foreigners to meet peacefully in this way is, under early conditions of society, not a light thing ; to insure the safety of all concerned, it is well that the spot should be under the protection of a god whom buyers and sellers alike will recognise. Herakles' adventures had won him the reputation of a great traveller, and it seems to have been thought that he would have a fellow-feeling even for less warlike and powerful wanderers than himself, the merchants who went up and down the country in early times. Also, he had a great reputation for averting evil of all kinds, as in his earthly life he had rid the world of many formidable beings who plagued it. At all events, in Italy he had become a protector of merchants, to whom they would dedicate a tithe of their profits in gratitude for his help. On occasion he was thought to disclose buried treasures also. So, since in many parts of the Greek world he was worshipped, not simply as a hero, or venerable and powerful ghost, but as a full-fledged god, Italian merchants seem to have adopted him as a patron, hence the erection of his altar on this trading-place. The cult is said to have been originally in the hands of two Roman clans, the Potitii and Pinarii, of whom the former had died out by the end of the Republic ; it was alleged that this extinction followed upon their impious selling of the secrets of the cult to State-owned slaves, at the instigation of Appius Claudius (one of a family of pestilent innovators), while he was censor in 312 B.C. At all events, the ritual was in the hands of the State officials from that time on ; it was Greek in character, the sacrifice was a heifer which had never been yoked, and the libation was made from an old wooden goblet said to have once belonged to Hercules himself. No other god might be mentioned during the rites, and the precinct was so holy that no dogs and no flies ever ventured to enter it. But Hercules was so little felt to be a foreigner that an Italian equivalent was found for him, in the person of an old and obscure god, Semo Sancus Dius Fidius.

A minor deity with a great future who was not of the

oldest stratum of Roman cult was Venus. Her name is curious ; by analogy with other nouns of like formation, it ought to be neuter, signifying something like "delightful appearance", which meant, not the beauty of women, but that of a piece of well-tilled ground, especially, it would seem, a vegetable-garden. At least, the dealers in vegetables and pot-herbs celebrated her festival on August 19th, the dedication-day of her temple. She cannot have been a very old importation, for Varro says he could find no mention of her in any ancient document ; but, for some reason now obscure, the idea grew up that she was the same as the Greek Aphrodite. Aphrodite in turn was the Greek name for the goddess anciently worshipped at Mt. Eryx in Sicily, and therefore this deity, around whose shrine a great deal of fighting went on in the first Punic War, was called in Latin Venus Erucina. Early in the second Punic War, when the presence of Hannibal with his invading army in Italy made men's minds very uneasy, a number of precautions were taken to secure the favour of all manner of gods, and one of these was a consultation of the Sibylline books (see p. 95), which advised that a temple be erected to this goddess. That was accordingly done, in 215 B.C., while another followed during the next century, in 181. It so happened that this latter shrine was founded on April 23rd, which was the day of the so-called Vinalia Priora, or earlier festival of wine, the day on which the grape-juice of the last year's vintage, having now fermented enough to be drinkable, was formally drawn and a libation of it poured out to Juppiter before any human lips tasted it, thus bringing the new, and therefore dangerous, liquid into contact with the wholesome *numen* of the god. It was not officially called wine (*uinum*) on that occasion, but *calpar*, a word which, to judge by its cognates in other languages than Latin, is derived from the name, not of the contents of the vessel used but of the vessel itself. It is a nice example of sacral caution. Wine is what men commonly drink, at least in a wine-making country ; until it has been made safe for drinking by the beneficent influence of Juppiter, it is safest to call it simply "that stuff in the pitcher". However, the coincidence of date gave rise to a common mistake ;

most people, although scholars and priests knew better, fancied that Venus was the goddess of the festival, and it became the day on which prostitutes made sacrifice to her. This is an example of undesirable foreign elements making their way into sober and decent Roman ritual ; some of the Oriental goddesses who were identified with Aphrodite, and therefore with Venus, had temple-harlots in their service, and the goddess of Eryx was one of them. A more respectable development, but still quite un-Roman, was the connexion between her and the great Julian family. They explained their name by saying that they were descended from a certain Iulus, son of Aeneas. But Aeneas (Aineias in Greek) was in mythology a son of Aphrodite ; in other words, the junior branch of the Trojan royal family, which seems to have survived the destruction of the city, was somehow associated with the local mother-goddess worshipped on Mt. Ida, near Troy. Therefore Aphrodite, or Venus, was the ancestress of that house which gave Rome its earlier Emperors, and from the time of Augustus on her cult was important. That Venus of Eryx in particular was honoured in this connexion was due to another development of Aeneas's legend, which credited him with founding her temple.

Other gods were Greek pure and simple, one at least not even changing his name when he came to Rome. This was Apollo, who was so widely worshipped in the Greek-speaking world that any nation in contact with Greek civilisation, even indirectly, was sure to hear of him. The Etruscan dynasty, like all Etruscans, had Greek contacts, by no means always friendly, and their people adopted the cult of so great a god quite early ; one of the most impressive monuments ancient Italy has left us is the famous statue of Apollo from Veii, a marvellous and awe-inspiring piece of Etruscan art, which shows the god at his most terrible. It is not surprising, therefore, that the Etruscan kings of Rome are represented as consulting the oracle at Delphoi on occasion, nor that they are credited with having acquired the Sibylline books for Rome. At quite an early date verses were current in Greece, supposed to be the inspired utterances of women known as Sibyls (*Sibyllai*), a word of unknown origin. That their inspiration came from Apollo was the generally received doctrine, for he tended to attach all diviners and prophets to himself by one means or another. One of these women was said to have lived, or even be still living, for she was credited with a life of 1,000 years, at Cumae, on the coast, not far west of Naples. Doubtless her legend and her prophecies had been brought by the Greek settlers in that part of Italy. A collection of verses supposed to be hers was in the possession of the Roman government from an early date, whether it was actually got by the Etruscan kings or not. It was kept in the Capitol, under the care of a priesthood whose duties extended to all new cults. They were the Two Commissioners for Ritual (*duouiri sacris faciundis*), whose numbers were increased till finally there were fifteen of them. Only they might consult the mysterious verses, and even they only by order of the secular authorities. Hence we know little of the contents of their collection, or of the later one which succeeded it, for Augustus got a new one together when he rebuilt the holy place, burned down during the civil wars between Marius and Sulla, in 83 B.C. He selected, from the many books offered from various quarters of the world, especially the supposed homes of the different Sibyls, those which he considered genuine, burned the rest, and stored the chosen prophecies, not in the Capitol, but in the base of the great statue of Apollo in his new temple on the Palatine, one of the most magnificent in Rome. For Augustus had a deep devotion, real or simulated, to Apollo and set up in his honour what was practically a rival cult to that of Juppiter, so that from this time onwards Roman official religion had two centres, one on each of the venerable heights overlooking the Forum. The older temple, however, lost little of its prestige, and was still the place to which, on the successful conclusion of a campaign, the triumphal procession made its way, though now it was always headed by a member of the Imperial house, as perpetual commander-in-chief ; a subject could get no more than the right to dress on formal occasions in the elaborate (originally royal) costume of one who had celebrated a triumph.

However, Apollo did not have to wait for the Empire

before being received and adequately housed in Rome. The immediate cause of his admission was perhaps some pestilence, for the oldest prayer to him of which we have any account was that uttered by the Vestals, and in this he was addressed as Physician and Healer (*Apollo medice, Apollo Paean*). Certainly he was called Physician in connexion with his oldest temple, vowed in 433 B.C. during a sickness and dedicated two years later. It stood outside the *pomerium*, near the river bank, and succeeded an older and smaller shrine. One of the new ceremonies of the second Punic War was the institution of games in his honour, which soon became annual. These in themselves were nothing new; Juppiter had long enjoyed a similar celebration, the Roman Games, made annual in 366 B.C., and the Plebeian Games were instituted about the same time as the Apolline, for they became annual in 216. But Apollo, being a Greek, liked Greek amusements, and his games were marked above others by the adoption of Greek dramatic performances, alongside of the Italian sports, the most characteristic of which were combats of gladiators. Actors, who were "Dionysos' craftsmen" in Greece, became "Apollo's guests" (*parasiti Apollinis*) in Rome, though they were also under the patronage of Minerva, like any other skilled workers. Their art, in its more serious forms, was never really popular, for even comedy, which had some quite good exponents during the second and third centuries B.C., languished afterwards and gave place to farce and ballet. One reason for this no doubt was that drama had no roots in the native religion, Etruria only having some few performances of a semi-dramatic character. The Greek states to the south did indeed have a certain amount of drama of their own, but never very highly developed; the inspiration of Roman dramatists in their more "legitimate" plays came from Greece proper.

Something has been said of the Greek cast which the worship of Ceres assumed (p. 72). Another Greek figure was that of Mercurius, or Mercury, as he is generally called in English. Like Hercules, he was a god of traders, and whatever his Italian origins may have been (it is not undisputed that he was ever a purely native god, and certainly he was not originally Roman), he came in that capacity, an important one belonging also to the Greek Hermes. He was an early importation, whatever the exact cause of his coming, for he was given a temple in 495 B.C., if our records are to be trusted for so ancient an event.

We know definitely when a later Greek figure arrived in Rome, the patron of physicians, Asklepios, whose name took the dialectical form Aesculapius in Roman mouths. His cult, as a great inhabitant of the underworld, who continued his healing activities mostly by means of visions granted to those who slept in his temples, was not widespread even in Greece till towards the end of the fifth century B.C., when it became extremely popular. About a century later, in 293 B.C., a pestilence was ranging in Rome, as commonly happened there, owing to the ill-planned and crowded streets and the general ignorance of hygiene. A Sibylline oracle advised them to seek the aid of Aesculapius, and a mission sent to Epidauros, one of his principal shrines, came back with a sacred serpent, a common enough epiphany of the deity. According to tradition, it slipped overboard as the ship with the ambassadors was coming up the Tiber, and landed on the island which stands in mid-stream opposite the mediaeval ghetto. Here a shrine was erected in honour of the god, and like many of his places of worship it became a sort of hospital or sanatorium ; Aesculapius was given Salus as his cult-partner, corresponding to Hygieia (Health) in his Greek cult, and to this day his influence may be said to continue, for the church and hospital of S. Bartolomeo now occupy the place. The island itself, in commemoration of the god's voyage, was given in antiquity the shape of a ship.

In 249 B.C., during the long-drawn first Punic War, when war-nerves were a common phenomenon, certain portents moved the Senate to authorise a consultation of the Sibylline books, and this time the advice was to hold games in honour of Pluto and Persephone (or, in Latin, with a translation of one name and a mispronunciation of the other, Dis and Proserpina) for three successive nights, and to repeat them once every *saeculum*, a period variously computed by the Etruscans, from whom it was derived, but generally fixed at either 100 or 110 years. This was duly done, at a place on the Campus Martius, in the northern part of Rome, called Tarentum, which, according to a natural conjecture of modern scholars, owed its name to the cult having originated in the Greek city of Tarentum (Greek Taras, now Taranto). The next celebration took place a little more than a century later, in 146 ; after a longer delay, Augustus celebrated the games in a new form, keeping up the nocturnal rites but adding brilliant shows on the corresponding days, in honour of Juppiter, Juno, Apollo and Diana. This was in 17 B.C., and justified by a highly artificial calculation of the dates when earlier periods had ended ; it was only to be expected that some of his successors did not wait for so long a time to elapse before celebrating so magnificent a ceremony and thus setting their own greatness on something like a level with his, but we need not go into the later occasions and the rival chronologies on which they were founded. It should be noted that in Imperial times the name of the festival was changed, and it was no longer called, as it had been, *ludi Tarentini* or games of Tarentum, but *ludi saeculares*, that is games marking a *saeculum*.

So much for actual Greek gods. A wider influence, however, than could be exercised merely by the reception of a few new cults was felt by about the third century B.C. A critical date is 217 B.C. It was apparently not unheard of in the native worship to have sacred feasts at which the deities were supposed to be present ; they were represented by bundles of herbs, known as "heads of gods". But in that year such a banquet was held (the Latin name for it is *lectisternium*, i.e. the preparing of couches such as diners reclined on by Greek custom), in honour of gods grouped in Greek fashion and represented by statues. On the first couch were Juppiter and Juno, husband and wife in the Greek identification of them as Zeus and Hera. On the next lay Neptune and Minerva, who to a Greek were Poseidon and Athena, the ancient deities of the Athenian akropolis. Then came Mars and Venus—Ares and Aphrodite were Greek cult-partners of long standing—Apollo and Diana (in Greek mythology, Apollo and Artemis are twins), then the two fire-deities, Volcanus and Vesta, finally two closely associated with the corn-trade, Ceres and Mercury. Only the last two groups make any reasonable sense if we start from the presuppositions of Roman cult ; the rest are pure Greek. From that time on we have abundant evidence of the growing Greek influence, both in cult and in every-day thought. Greek myths are assumed as known in dramatic authors, and attached to Roman deities equated with Greek ones. Old groupings begin to break up ; thus Saturn, who was identified with Kronos, presumably because of the resemblance between their festivals, was paired no longer with Lua but with Ops, whom some freak of theology interpreted as Kronos' consort, Rhea. Consus, her real cult-partner, was not easily identified with any Greek god (some guessed wildly that, since his altar lay in the Circus, and horse-races were held there, he must be Poseidon, Lord of Steeds), and so, like several other such deities, retired into the background. The vague old figures became clear-cut personalities of the Greek type, and Greek statues, or imitations of them, housed in temples built after the Greek pattern, were more and more to be seen all over Rome and Italy.

It was unfortunate that these once bright Olympian figures came to be widely known at a time when they were losing their lustre for their originators. The failure of the traditional deities of Greece to preserve the city-states which had long worshipped them was causing much religious unrest,[1] with tendencies towards individualism in worship, a search for new and more satisfactory cults, and an abundant crop of theories, some of a decidedly skeptical nature. One of the shallowest of these, that of Euhemeros (fourth and third centuries B.C.) was taken up in Rome not long after its author's own day by Ennius (239-169), the greatest of those writers who made Greek literary methods familiar to Rome. His Latin translation or adaptation of Euhemeros' romance, in which under the form of a traveller's tale he set forth his theory that the traditional gods were kings and other noteworthy persons, deified after their death by admirers or flatterers, made far more impression in Rome than

[1] See *Ancient Greek Religion*, p. 100.

it ever had in Greece, because the Romans seldom had either a philosophical or a historical training such as would have helped them to detect the weaknesses of such a doctrine. About a century later, the view held, for instance, by Polybios the historian, as it had been by sundry others before him, gained some ground ; it was, that religion in general was nothing but a deep political scheme devised by early rulers and moralists to awe their subjects into good behaviour when human devices for detecting and punishing their irregularities were not likely to succeed. Hence, together with the very cults which in their hey-day might have added vividness and variety to the sober but rather dull native religion, came tendencies to disregard all religion, except for the maintaining of the State ceremonies which were part of the machinery of government. The last two centuries of the Republic saw a decline, becoming more and more rapid, of religion in Rome, and with it the loss of a good deal of what the Romans called *religio*, the scrupulosity which had once marked their conduct and led, among other things, to such excellent results as a careful keeping of sworn obligations. No doubt much unenlightened feeling and not a little sheer superstition was got rid of in this period, but it is to be doubted if the average educated man of the age of Cicero was either on such a high level morally or so likely to develop for himself a religion or a philosophy which could guide his conduct as his ancestor of some two hundred years earlier had been. It was a weakness of the Roman mind that in most departments of knowledge not immediately connected with the needs of everyday life and the necessary carrying out of routine public duties they were far too prone to adopt Greek conclusions ready-made and too little able to criticise them radically, or to form any fresh opinions for themselves. Hence it is that there never was a Roman school of philosophy in any proper sense of the word (teachers of philosophy and groups of persons interested in it did exist), nor any Roman science, unless it be jurisprudence.

One idea taken over from Greece was that gratitude for benefits constituted a good reason for paying divine honours. Since the gods were traditionally the givers of good things,

if good things came from any source, that indicated the presence of something like deity. This, properly understood and
followed out, might have led to a form of religion by no
means degraded ; what it actually caused was not only such
a theory as that of Euhemeros but strange freaks of cult.
Plutarch has a story of "the man who sacrificed an ox to his
benefactor", and can give the name of the sacrificer ; one
Pyrrhias of Ithake thus honoured an old man who had made
him rich in return for a great service. The remarkable thing
about this folk-tale, for such it undoubtedly is, is that
Plutarch, a pious and learned man, shows no signs of blaming
Pyrrhias for his eccentric way of showing gratitude. Much
more important was the quite common deification of men
of high rank, especially kings of the Hellenistic kingdoms
which sprang up in the ruins of Alexander the Great's empire.
This was most commonly done after their deaths, but not
infrequently in their lives, and to speak of a reigning prince,
directly or by implication, as a god was a commonplace of
courtly language. Hellenistic philosophy, too, held that to be
truly royal a man must have in him something which exceeded
ordinary humanity.[1] Another development belonging to this
period is the occasional cult of an abstraction ; thus it is said
that Timoleon, the Corinthian patriot to whom Syracuse also
owed a temporary freedom from illegal absolutism, is said to
have had a private chapel to Automatia, or "that which
happens of itself", in commemoration of the good fortune
which had attended his most daring undertakings.

All these tendencies are reflected, at one time or another,
in Roman cult. Abstract qualities, which were rarely worshipped in Greece, though to personify them is one of the
commonest figures of speech in their poetry, enjoyed much
veneration in Rome. One reason for this is probably that the
average Roman had little power of abstraction, as is shown
by the comparative rarity of abstract nouns in the language.
It has been ingeniously suggested that the origin of such
words is not the philosophical process of seeing and naming
a quality which many things have in common, but rather the
belief in a supernatural power which gives certain qualities,

[1] Cf. *Ancient Greek Religion*, p. 102.

and there is little doubt that this is true in some cases. Fear, for example, under its Greek name, Phobos, has not the form of an abstract noun at all, and the evidence is fairly cogent that the word meant originally a supernatural being who made men take fright and run away in battle. Good Faith (Fides) is quite an ancient divinity in Rome, her cult being ascribed to Numa ; that is to say, no record existed of a time when she was not worshipped. She was associated with Juppiter, naturally enough, since the sky-god, who sees all that men do, is everywhere a favourite witness to oaths and treaties, and the three senior *flamines*, that is the very core of the oldest clergy, in the service of the three principal gods of the most ancient State cult, used yearly to go to her shrine on the Capitol and offer sacrifice. Juventas was another dweller on the Capitol and associated with Juppiter ; she watched over the *iuuenes*, the men of military age, from the time they put on the men's toga till they were too old to be liable to army service. A few more old deities were of like kind, and it seems a very natural way of expressing the presence, actual or hoped for, of some special kind of *numen* to attach such a name to it. But in the later period which we are discussing, cults of abstractions pure and simple sprang up thickly. When Concord (Concordia) was first given a temple by the great M. Furius Camillus, in 367 B.C., no doubt she was still the author of that *numen* which made all Romans hold together in times of stress. But when L. Opimius restored it in 121 B.C., to commemorate the end of the disturbances due to the Gracchi and their abortive reforms, we may suspect the intrusion of a more abstract idea, such as might in later time have expressed itself in an allegorical painting or statue, while we need have no doubt that the future emperor Tiberius, when he re-dedicated it to Concordia Augusta, in A.D. 10, was simply personifying the good relations between the members of the Imperial house. Cults of Concordia now grew up all over the Empire, often with titles added to show what particular sort of agreement or "team spirit" was meant. Yet more certainly abstract was Clementia Augusta, who reflected the mercy which the Emperors, some of them with justification, claimed as a corner-stone of their policy. A cult

directed to a colourless figure of this kind was a respectable
way of issuing official propaganda or of displaying decorous
loyalty, and hardly more.

If we wish to understand how little deification might
mean, from the point of view of any reasonable theology,
we cannot do better than to examine the correspondence of
Cicero after the death of his beloved daughter Tullia. He
was a man of strong family affections, and she apparently
was an amiable woman, who probably returned his natural
feeling for her. We are well acquainted with his views on
philosophical matters; he was an Academic, which meant
much the same as an agnostic. Certainly he had no deep
convictions concerning the destiny of human beings after
their death, still less a persuasion that his daughter had
become something superhuman and powerful on leaving her
body. Yet he cherished the intention to erect nothing less
than a temple to her. Several letters to his closest friend,
Atticus, treat of the matter ; he busied himself with choosing
a suitable site for the building, and reiterated that it was not
to be a tomb or funeral monument of any kind, but a shrine
(*fanum*) which could not be mistaken for anything else and
should be respected as such by later owners of the ground
on which it was to stand.

"It is a shrine I want", he declares, "and I won't give up the
idea. I am anxious to avoid any likeness to a tomb, not so much
because of the legal penalty [on excessive expenditure upon funerals]
as because I must have as near as possible a deification" (or apothe-
osis ; he uses the Greek word).

If therefore a tender-hearted man's somewhat extravagant
but natural and genuine grief could find such an expression
as this, we need not wonder that when a really great states-
man like Augustus did immense good to the general welfare
by putting an end to the continual civil brawls, which often
rose to devastating wars between rival parties, and establishing a stable and not oppressive government, many were
perfectly ready to worship him, and he even had to check
a tendency which was repugnant to some of his Italian
subjects, not because they thought it blasphemous—that was

a Jewish and later a Christian reaction to the prevalent
Emperor-worship—but because it was not Roman, and conservatism was a force to be reckoned with. Two motives
seem to have inspired those who kept up the cult of him
and many of his successors. To some, it was a recognized
means of showing gratitude and loyalty ; many established
gods were nothing but men to whom such an honour had
been paid in the past, and Augustus was quite as good as
any of them. To others, what they were worshipping was the
divine element really existing in Augustus, which in due
course would depart to its proper place in heaven. That is
what the poets of the time say, adding that they hope the
departure will be long delayed ; and what is a piece of
dutiful metaphor to them, was probably plain fact to the
minds of many plain people. In Italy, the official compromise
was to worship his genius. Whatever the genius may originally
have been, by that time it was the spiritual double of a man,
which came into and passed out of this world with him, ruled
his life and was pleased if he enjoyed himself ; to "indulge
the genius" is to eat, drink and be merry, while to "cheat
the genius" is to live miserly. But throughout, the genius
remained divine, a proper object of worship for a man and
all his household, and therefore in the case of the genius
of one who received the title of "father of his country", a
very proper being for his "children" to adore. Once Augustus,
or any popular Emperor, was dead, Graeco-Roman sentiment
was well satisfied if he was formally declared to be divine
and so given a cult and priests as the latest addition to the
hierarchy of gods, for nothing in ancient belief obliged anyone to suppose that the deities formed a close corporation
to which no one else might ever be admitted. However, it
should be clearly recognised that this practice of deification
and all that it implied were an importation from the Greek
world. It is instructive to listen to Cicero once more, speaking,
no longer as a bereaved father, but as a Roman senator, and
discussing the proposal to give divine honours to Julius
Caesar.

Conscript fathers, do you think that I would have moved what
you unwillingly voted for, to blend funeral ceremonies with prayers,

to bring into the commonwealth a pollution past atonement, to enact that we should pray to a dead man ? I say nothing of what man it was. Let it be Lucius Brutus, who himself rid the State of kingly tyranny and whose posterity, after nearly five centuries, display the like valour by the like deeds ; even so I could not be brought to let any dead man intrude into the awful presence of the immortal gods, or allow the State to worship one whose tomb is there to receive the rites of the departed.

We thus find, by the end of the Republic, a strange unreality in Roman religion. The ancient festivals and many new ones subsisted, indeed were often popular, for one of the chief means of marking them was to hold public shows, including the ever-welcome displays of gladiatorial combats and fights with wild beasts. Most of the old priesthoods remained in existence, though not all ; the office of flamen Dialis, with its burdensome tabus, was vacant for seventy-five years after the death of its last Republican holder, in 87 B.C. Matters of ritual remained under the control of the pontiffs, who often were asked their advice and by whose authority not a few ceremonies were added, altered or forbidden. The position of augur remained respectable and sought after ; the list of members of that venerable college includes the names of Sulla the dictator, Pompey the Great, Hortensius and Cicero the orators, Mark Antony, Julius Caesar and other leading men. It is interesting to remember that of these, Caesar was an Epicurean and therefore believed neither that the gods were interested in what happened in this world nor that they sent signs of any kind, while Cicero kept an open mind on divination, inclining towards disbelief. But many temples had fallen into ruin or were left unrestored after accident or the ravages of war had destroyed them. Such opinions as are expressed in surviving documents bear testimony to the sheer ignorance of even the best-informed as to the true characteristics of the national cult. Religious machinery was freely used for sordid ends in the endless political squabbles. False swearing was a commonplace. The whole atmosphere of the educated classes was one of indifference to religion, combined with a polite observance of such of its forms as were at once traditional in public life

and not particularly burdensome. Yet the following generations saw a great and growing interest in such things, and
from two to four centuries later the best minds in the Empire
were deeply concerned, not simply with questions of conduct,
but with mystic experiences, minute points of theology, and
controversies between one highly transcendental faith and
another. It shall be the task of the following chapter to try
and trace some at least of the causes of this remarkable change.

CHAPTER IV

AUGUSTUS AND THE REVIVAL
OF RELIGION

THE adopted son of Julius Caesar, Octavian, or, as he
subsequently was called, Augustus, was one of the greatest
and most astute statesmen ever born. Coming to manhood
in the midst of civil commotion, at the end of some three-
quarters of a century of increasing disturbance, he left behind
him at the close of his long life an ordered State which,
despite the follies and vices of not a few of his successors
and many of their underlings, withstood all strains for over
three hundred years, during which occurred the longest
periods of peace that Europe had ever known or has seen
since. In theory, what he had done was to restore the Republic
in its best and most enlightened form. To quote his own
words, from the memorandum of his achievements which
he caused to be inscribed in several parts of his Empire :

In my sixth and seventh consulates, having put an end to civil
wars and being by universal consent in supreme control, I handed
over the commonwealth from my own power to the good pleasure
of the Senate and People of Rome. . . . Thereafter, although
I enjoyed greater prestige than my fellow-magistrates, I had no
ampler powers than theirs.

All, therefore, was supposedly as it had been before, and

Rome governed herself through the traditional and constitutional machinery inherited from the past, while paying attention, as many political thinkers had been urging her to do for a century or more, to the advice and example of her leading citizen, the *princeps* or chief man, to whom, incidentally, it had been found expedient to delegate for the time being certain extraordinary powers. Whether anyone seriously believed this formula we may well doubt ; but that it was the ostensible basis of the early Empire is quite certain. The detail that the "chief citizen" had under his hand the entire military and naval forces of the State was judiciously kept in the background, and it was an evil day for Rome when it became no longer a secret that any Emperor owed his security to them. Augustus was content with real power ; later rulers wanted and ultimately got both the substance and form of absolutism.

From early in his career, the new monarch surrounded himself with a halo of religious veneration. His title, given him by the Senate, carefully avoided everything other than that, and though Greeks frankly referred to him and his successors as kings (*basilês*) no Roman ever called them anything of the kind. The word *augustus* means him or that in which something, namely *numen*, is increased ; its first two syllables are identical with *augur* (see p. 85). Long before the first and greatest holder of the title was born, Ennius had spoken of an *augustum augurium*, a sign of divine approval, heavily charged with *numen*, which had authorised the foundation of Rome. It was therefore in keeping with his position that one of his principal tasks was to restore, not only the ancient morality of his people and their old and deep-seated respect for law and order, but their religion. To this end he revived half-forgotten priesthoods, saw to it that candidates for such posts as those of the Vestal Virgins and the various flaminates were forthcoming, built or re-built temples in many places, but especially in Rome, inaugurated new worships, as that of the Palatine Apollo (cf. p. 95), and himself eagerly accepted the post of chief pontiff as soon as it became vacant by the death of his former colleague and rival, Lepidus, who had fallen into complete political insignificance but was scrupulously spared to perform such of the duties attached to his holy office as he chose to fulfil. Religion became respectable and, what was at least as important, loyal. The greatest poem of the generation before, that of Lucretius, had taught Epicureanism and thundered against the degrading superstition which made men think that the gods could be angry with them, or indeed cared in the least what they did or how they fared. The greatest poets of Augustan date vary between the outspoken remark of Ovid that it is expedient to have gods and therefore we should think that they exist, and the profound piety of Vergil. How sincere Augustus himself was is a question which is never likely to be answered ; it is, however, possible to see what materials he had to work upon and to what extent he made his Romans what they once had been, the most scrupulously pious of mankind.

It must in the first place be noted that no strongly anti-religious feeling existed anywhere. The uneducated went on with their traditional practices, or such of them as survived, especially the old-established rites of the country-side, and, we may suppose, entertained vague and uncritical beliefs corresponding to them. Among the educated, there were many who had no religious beliefs, but few if any who objected to religion existing or would do anything actively to oppose it. Most Romans, if they took an interest in philosophy at all, were either Stoics or Epicureans ; probably the numbers of both had grown considerably in the last half-century or so, for while in Cicero we catch something of the tones of a missionary making an unfamiliar doctrine known, in Augustan writers it seems to be assumed that most people have at least a general knowledge of the tenets of the principal philosphers. Of these schools, the Epicureans taught that gods existed, and had the outward appearance familiar from art and literature, but that their abode was outside not only this universe (we should say "solar system") but the innumerable others which they postulated as existing. They had not created anything, they were not troubled with the moral or other government of any of the worlds ; being perfectly happy, they had no onerous duties of any kind, but lived in a blissful state of contemplation, apparently of their own perfections and bliss. Yet they may have had a certain passive and involuntary influence. It has been acutely pointed out by Dr. Bailey[1] that Epicurean religion (he is speaking of the more thoughtful Epicureans) was a contemplative adoration of these beings, and that, according to one of the recorded utterances of Epicurus (341-270 B.C.) himself, the emanations from their divine bodies were productive of much good. For Epicureanism allowed of no realities which were not corporeal, distinguishing merely between grosser and finer material substances. The ideas men have of the gods are due to the impinging on the substance of the human mind of a kind of very tenuous shells of fine matter which, being continually thrown off the bodies of the gods, as off every other object, make their way through the intervening space and reach our senses in a more or less undamaged condition. These fragments, therefore, of beings perfect in every way, might greatly improve a receptive human adorer by putting into him something of a nature far superior to humanity. Hence a consistent Epicurean might well do as the founder of the school had done and take part in the conventional and established worship of his country, while retaining his own opinions of the nature of the beings to which it was addressed and the efficaciousness or otherwise of the rites used.

The Stoics, on the other hand, came by a very different route to a not dissimilar result, as indeed was the case in many matters of ordinary conduct. Their philosophy was deterministic, teaching that everything was minutely fore-ordained by an all-wise and benevolent Providence. Furthermore, they laid great stress on the validity of universal customs and beliefs ; this was one of their reasons for holding divination to be a real science, for there is no people on earth which has not some way of trying to foretell the future. Where a popular practice or story appeared to be childish or immoral, they were very ready to discover in it some profound allegory, and especially to allegorise the popular gods, largely by extremely bad puns of the sort which then

[1] *Phases, &c.* (see Bibliography), p. 225 and notes.

passed for etymologies. Since the universe and all its parts are divine (Stoicism has been described as a materialistic pantheism), many of the gods fitted at once into their places in the Stoic scheme. The chief deities, says Varro, voicing Stoic doctrine as he usually does, are Heaven and Earth. Now Juppiter is the heavens or the air ; therefore Juno, being his wife, is Earth ; she is called Queen because she rules over all earthly things. The sun and moon are plainly divine ; but the sun is Apollo (this is an older theory than Stoicism, for it goes back to the fifth century B.C., and Stoicism is of the third), and Artemis, who is the same as Diana, is the moon. In this way every god could somehow be brought into the wide net of their doctrine and regarded as nothing but a popular presentation of their philosophy. Therefore the originators of the conventional cults had been good Stoics, whether they knew it or not, and consequently there could be no possible objection to participating in the rites their ancient wisdom had established for the guidance of posterity.

The two principal schools, then, to one or the other of which most educated Romans of the day attached themselves, were not likely to offer any opposition to a restored and augmented cult of the State deities. There was another, of some importance towards the close of the Republic, which would be still less inclined to object. This was neo-Pythagoreanism, a curious mixture of philosophy, mysticism and magic which found its adepts in Rome. They possibly included Nigidius Figulus, the most learned man, except Varro, of the last generation of the Republic, but better known to later times as an astrologer and diviner. However, they were more prominent in connexion with a certain Quintus Sextius, head of a short-lived and unoriginal school of Roman thought, who blended some Pythagorean elements with his Stoicism and was succeeded by his son and a few other disciples. Sextius himself was a contemporary of Julius Caesar, and the best-known Roman to be influenced by him and his followers was the younger Seneca, tutor of the emperor Nero and one of his victims. Such men would certainly not oppose a movement intended to restore the ancient pieties of the country, especially as it went with a serious attempt to bring back the moral principles which the earlier Republic, not undeservedly, was credited with observing.

Among the unphilosophical part of the public, which was always greatly in the majority, there were some at least who cared for the arts, and to them no doubt the appearance of many handsome temples and good statues was welcome. The Augustan cult was a splendid one, and may be assumed to have gained some popularity for that reason. A further influence in its favour was the genuine feeling which many had that divine events were taking place. The poets, as so often, reflect this, and interpret it in their own way. No poem of Vergil's is more famous than the fourth Eclogue. In this extraordinary and beautiful composition, included in his collection of pastorals but explicitly striking a higher note than the rest, he hails the coming of a new and better time, which presently, although not at once, shall bring back the primal innocence and happiness of mankind, Hesiod's Golden Age, the "reign of Kronos" of Greek popular tradition. A child is to be born, the son of a great but human father, who shall rule the world, see the Iron Age disappear after the last wars have been fought (and even they shall have the character of noble exploits, marking a return to the Heroic Age of Hesiod's series), and attain to the society of gods. What child and what parents he means, and what his materials were—he himself names a Sibylline prophecy, but we know no details—are highly controversial points. Of the general meaning there is no doubt ; all things are to be made new, by divine help. The date of this poem is 40 B.C., not very long before the establishment of Octavian's power by the defeat of his great rival Antony in 31. There are in fact some indications, though confused and doubtful after the lapse of time and because of the imperfect state of our documentation, that the end of an age, a *saeculum* of some kind, was indeed expected about then by some people. One form of this belief is reflected in a story told by that ancient commentator on Vergil who is traditionally called Daniel's Servius, in memory of Pierre Daniel, the scholar who first published him. A certain Etruscan diviner, when the comet which startled the general public by appearing at the time of Julius Caesar's funeral games was attracting attention, declared that it marked the end of the ninth and the beginning of the tenth *saeculum* of his traditional system. He added that the gods were not willing to have this secret revealed, and would show their displeasure by his immediate death ; and there and then, before he could finish what he was saying to the assembled people, he dropped dead. Whether or not this particular event ever happened is a small matter ; the important fact is that sometime about the date of Octavian's rise to power and the conferring on him of his great title such feelings as gave rise to the fiction, if it is one, were not uncommon. But the doctrine of ages of the world, each of which has its own characteristics, good or bad, is in its origin a piece of Oriental mysticism. The existence, there-fore, of such a belief and the quest for signs of the end of one period and the beginning of another and better one were essentially religious phenomena. The holders of such beliefs expected supernatural powers of some kind, gods new or old, stars (for astrology was daily gaining influence) or some impersonal but superhuman fate, to bring about the change. It was never supposed to come about through natural and historical causes, such as the enactment of new and better laws or the improvements in government which the merely human wisdom of able statesmen might suggest.

There are, moreover, indications that conjectures were rife as to what power was going to intervene and improve the state of the world. Vergil declares openly that Apollo is now reigning, implying that he is at least the initiator of the new Golden Age. Horace, in an ode written probably not very long after Vergil's poem, certainly before Actium (31 B.C.), after painting a direful picture of the portents which proclaim the wrath of heaven against Rome for the sins of the civil wars, culminating in the murder of Caesar, asks what deity will rescue the nation, and hesitates between Apollo, Venus, Mars and Mercury, implying that the last-named has taken human shape, that of Octavian, and will bring about, not a new age, but a return to more prosperous times and better relations with Heaven. All four of these are connected in one way or another with the Imperial house, especially the first two ; and since Horace was himself a man not particularly interested in religious affairs, certainly no pietist, it is a reasonable supposition that he is reflecting in poetical language thoughts which were in the heads of some at least of his fellow Romans.

Augustus, then, whatever other motives he may have had and whatever may have been his personal beliefs, was using an existing current of feeling which looked and hoped for an era of prosperity due to divine favour expressing itself in and through him and his family. That this should take the form of increased attention to the outward expressions of worship, priesthoods, temples and magnificent festivals, was inevitable, seeing that the revival had governmental authority behind it. The hopes of his contemporaries were to be a considerable extent fulfilled, for he did succeed in establishing a workable system of government for the Empire, removing many of the most glaring abuses, and at least making personal respectability among the members of Roman fashionable society a thing not to be set at naught, as it often had been in the immediately preceding generations. One thing is fairly certain concerning him, that he believed strongly in his personal luck or destiny, a not uncommon characteristic of men who have risen quickly to high power ; it will be re- membered that it was found in an extreme form in Hitler. In Rome, such a belief had been quite characteristic of several prominent adventurers. Sulla had styled himself Felix in Latin, Epaphroditos in Greek, both surnames meaning "lucky". Julius Caesar's one outstanding belief seems to have been trust in his fortune ; a famous story concerning him is that he cheered the master of a small vessel in rough weather by assuring him that he had "Caesar and his luck for shipmates" and so would come to no harm. In the case of Augustus, the belief took an astrological form, character- istic of the times. According to Suetonius, he consulted an astrologer and, being persuaded to give particulars of the time of his birth, was astonished to see the expert spring up from his seat and prostrate himself before him.

"Thereafter," adds the biographer, "Augustus had such con- fidence in his destiny that he published the scheme of his nativity and stamped an issue of silver coinage with the sign Capricorn, under which he was born".

Actually, he was not born but conceived when Capricorn was on the eastern horizon and therefore his horoscope-sign ; he was born under Libra. But Capricorn is a royal sign, therefore better suited to his ambitions, careful though he was never to style himself king.

Here it may be well to explain briefly the strange pseudo-science of astrology (commonly known in antiquity as *mathesis*, "the learning", i.e., the science *par exellence*, and its practitioners as *mathematici* from their subject or *Chaldaei* from the country of its origin). It depends upon the theory, generally received by ancient astronomers, which puts the earth in the centre of the solar system, and consequently the general acceptance of the Copernican cosmography marked the end of it in educated belief. Since the rays of the seven planets of ancient astronomy (Saturn, Jupiter, Mars, the Sun, Venus, Mercury, the Moon, in the order of their relative distances, real or supposed, from the earth), naturally fall upon the centre of the system, that is to say on the earth's surface, and since they are divine, or instruments of destiny, or at all events capable of influencing whatever they shine upon, it follows that they must determine the lives and fortunes of those who are born under them, in other words of every human being, to say nothing of other animals. How they determine it is a matter of calculation, for the potency of any planet varies according to its position in the sky at a given moment, relative to the earth itself and to the other planets, also to the signs of the zodiac. Every planet has its house, the sign (sometimes more than one) in which it is in familiar and friendly surroundings, also its exaltation, the position at which it has its maximum power, its depression or humiliation (*tapeinoma* in Greek), which is the position of its minimum power, and furthermore, it may be the horo-scope, that is to say exactly on the eastern horizon at the time of the birth (or conception) of the child in question, or at the zenith or nadir (in Latin *summum caelum*, *imum caelum*), or in some other significant position. But the signs of the zodiac also have each its potency ; for instance, a child born under Aquarius, that is to say when some degree of the constellation of that name is horoscope, will have a life in some way connected with water ; he may for example be a fisherman or sailor, or a skilful swimmer, or he may die by drowning, according to the other features of his scheme of nativity, in other words the position of the heavenly bodies at his birth. By combining the indications of the planets with those of the signs and, to a lesser degree, those furnished by other constellations than the ones included in the zodiac, all possible destinies may be worked out with considerable minuteness. The rules, in time, grew to such an extreme complication that an astrologer had always a loophole of escape if his predictions were too flagrantly falsified ; some obscure detail of observation or calculation might have been overlooked, or the exact moment of birth not have been rightly given, or one of the many and conflicting authorities have misled him on some essential point. On the whole, their forecasts gained much credence, so much so indeed that they were often discouraged by the State ; clearly, it would be dangerous if some ambitious subject were told that his nativity destined him to be king, and enquiries as to the exact length of days allotted to the reigning Emperor were much too close akin to a plot against his life to be looked upon with any complacency. Theoretical arguments against astrology, enforced by examples of its failure (including the recurrent one, that twins do not always lead the same kind of life) were common, and were eagerly taken up by Christian apologists, for the Church always officially opposed astrology, though with indifferent success. Arguments on the other side were not lacking ; for instance, the argument of the twins could be countered by the celebrated answer attributed to Nigidius Figulus, in explanation of his surname, which means "the potter". Setting a potter's wheel in motion, he flicked it twice in rapid succession with a paintbrush, and then stopped it. The marks were far apart. He then pointed out that the heavens moved much faster than the wheel, and so the time between the birth of one twin and another would be more than enough to give them a different scheme of nativity, and therefore different destinies. Astrology also appealed in a varying degree to literary men, and one, a versifier of considerable ability named Manilius, contemporary with Augustus and his successor Tiberius, has left us five books of clever hexameters on the subject. With eloquence and a show of reason on both sides, the controversy went on till long after the close of antiquity, until at last the heliocentric theory of the universe, when its truth could no longer be doubted, left it impossible to imagine the influences of the heavenly bodies converging on a moving earth which was no longer in the centre for them to converge upon.

But astrology was in its origin the fruit of Mesopotamian worship of the heavenly bodies, and therefore religious in its nature. That the stars were divine was a doctrine taught by several philosophic schools, and therefore most of those who accepted astrology perforce took up an attitude towards the phenomena of the skies which was not naturalistic, or not wholly so. As time went on, astral worship concentrated, so to speak, chiefly in the cult of the sun, which was not altogether foreign to Italy, since the Sun and Moon appear, though not prominently, among the ancient deities of the City. It was encouraged by two strong influences, that of oriental cults, of which we shall have to speak later, and a growing tendency of theologians to explain traditional divinities as either solar or lunar, generally the former, which in late antiquity was so widespread that Macrobius (flourished about A.D. 400) declares almost all gods are equated with the sun.

Almost a corollary of astrology was magic. In a simple form this was native to Rome ; Chapter I has given us examples of ancient rites which seem to have been intended not so much to induce a god to exercise his *numen* in the desired direction as to get hold of a sufficient supply of it for the operators to use for their immediate purposes. The Twelve Tables, the most ancient Roman code of laws, forbade two forms at least of sorcery, the use of a noxious charm, *malum carmen* (which, by a quaint misinterpretation of later lawyers, was taken to mean a defaming poem, and so gave rise to a law of libel) and the practice of making a neighbour's crops leave his fields and come magically to those of the sorcerer. But a new and more learned era of magic was now in full bloom. It was an ancient belief, widespread and in no wise confined to the speakers of the two classical languages, that gods could be induced by a moderate amount of prayer and sacrifice to remit the penalties due even to great sins. The stars, divine or not, were seldom thought to be so easily entreated ; they went on their unchanging courses, and their influences were exerted on all alike. Hence the desire to get somehow out of range of their powers. Their influence moved from the heavens inward, hence it did not affect the gods, whose seat was above the stars. Obviously, man could not rise to such heights himself, at least not in this life, though here and there doctrines of Greek or Oriental origin found converts according to which after death the soul might pass through successive stages of advancement until it finally became a god. Such a destiny, however, was not for the ordinary run of mankind, whose virtues were not so lofty as to deserve such promotion. But magic might hope to give the adept power over, at least, some of the lesser beings in the long series which led up to true godhead. For, in the magicians' creed, which was not theirs only, every god was at the head of an elaborate series of *daimones*, or supernatural powers which, though less than divine, were considerably more than human, and moreover was in sympathy with a section of the universe, working down through heavenly bodies to earthly ones, till finally it ended in a plant or other familiar object. Thus it was possible to get into touch with a deity by performing the proper rites on a particular flower, or the like, and the process was vastly facilitated by knowing the proper, that is the mystical or magic, names of every- thing and everyone concerned. Therefore a powerful and expert sorcerer could bring himself into contact with a being so great that no star and no fate had power over him, and so, as it were, take the whole apparatus of mortal destiny in rear. Such ambitious sorceries, however, do not seem to have been greatly credited in Italy, where foreign magic, although it was not uncommon, appears to have dealt largely in elaborate curses, by which all manner of powers were pressed into service for such things as lovers' quarrels and the disabling of horses against which the curser wished to bet, or in the harmless performances of herbalists, whose simples were made potent by being gathered at the astrologically right moments and under the appropriate magical auspices. Fortune-telling by magical means was common enough, and included necromancy ; some accused particular wizards of killing human victims, either because their entrails gave surer signs of the divine will than those of the lower animals, or to make potent charms out of parts of their bodies, or to press their ghosts into service. But it was regularly foreign practitioners who were supposed to perform such doubtful rites as these. Thessalian women had a great reputation for witchcraft ; it is a diviner from Armenia or Kommagene who, in Juvenal, will consult the entrails of a murdered boy if those of a fowl do not tell him enough ; later, Simon Magus of Samaria is supposed to have used the soul of a child he had put to death for his wonders. It is probably largely a matter of climate that the documents relating to sorcery which we have come from Egypt, where papyrus will keep indefinitely in the dry air, but the impression gathered from the evidence that we have is that Romans and Italians generally neither practised magic much themselves nor lent the names of their native deities to it ; the Egyptian books of magic and other sources of information show us a miscellaneous throng of Greek, Egyptian, Asiatic and newly invented supernatural beings whose names, together with curious combinations of meaningless letters, are used as words of power. Magic was on the whole a disreputable thing in the capital, at least until later times than those of Augustus.

But other ways of putting the individual into touch with divinity were not unpopular. As usually happens when a state grows large and complex, the ordinary man or woman was apt to feel inferior and powerless, the plaything of forces in this world and the other which were much too strong to be resisted. The reaction to this was naturally of different kinds for different temperaments. The Stoic saint (for that sect did not lack them, as it also had martyrs to boast of) found comfort in perfect acquiescence to perfect wisdom. The fates, says the Stoics' best-known Latin exponent, Seneca, lead the willing but drag the unwilling. Peace of mind was to be had by meditation on the truths of philosophy, especially the central dogma of Stoic ethics, that there is nothing good save virtue, nothing bad save vice, all else being indifferent ; wherefore a perfectly good man, a Stoic ideal sage, is the equal of a god, for the circumstance that the god lives for ever, or at least a whole world-age, and the sage does not, makes no moral difference, and so is of no account. Their finest poet, the lovable young satirist Persius, has a lofty conception of worship, which is also good Stoic, as might be expected. He hates ostentation and extravagance, "what is gold doing in a holy place ?" and holds that the most acceptable gift is a pure heart,

"justice and piety blended in the soul, holiness in the inmost parts of the bosom, a noble heart deep dyed in righteousness. Give me these offerings for our temples, and coarse meal will be acceptable sacrifice enough."

At the same time, Stoicism preached as a duty the taking of an active part in public affairs if opportunity arose. It was unfortunate that many of its exponents were so imbued with a sentimental republicanism that, besides their creditable protests against the misdoings of bad Emperors, they were at times guilty of factious opposition to good ones, and thus brought philosophy in general, as well as their own school, into disfavour. Despite the part, judicious and otherwise, which they thus played from time to time in the affairs of the State (their most famous public man was of course the Emperor M. Aurelius Antoninus), Stoicism was a strongly individual philosophy, and its chief aim was the good of the individual's soul.

If there were philosophers who thus made their philosophy very nearly a religion, there were religious sects with a tinge of philosophy. The Roman state as a rule persecuted no one's belief ; even its attitude towards Christianity is not really an exception to this. But it had a deep-seated dislike to anything resembling a secret society, and its experience of secret religious rites had not been encouraging. In 186 B.C., the Senate had felt obliged to take swift and stern action against an outbreak of Dionysiac mysteries over a great part of Italy. According to the official account, preserved in substance by Livy, while the text of the actual decree has come down to us, the movement started from Etruria, which had proved a fruitful ground for the missionary activities of an obscure Greek priest of the cult. Under his guidance, initiations at first of a few, later of considerable numbers of both sexes began to take place, and under cover of the excitable religion of their god[1] the adepts began to indulge in immoralities and offences of all sorts ; so at least it was alleged, and it is unlikely that we shall ever know what proportion of mere scandal and gossip and what percentage of real fact underlay the accusations. The State, which had abundant machinery for suppressing foreign and unauthorised cults, put it promptly into force, thus getting rid, according still to the official apologists, of the makings of a dangerous conspiracy not only against private morals but against public authority. Henceforth any persons whose conscience bade them worship Dionysos must get permission to do so, perform their ceremonies without secrecy, and allow only a small number to be present, unless special leave was granted.

This, however, was very far from being the end of secret or semi-secret worships in Italy. In the nature of things, we do not know a great deal about them, for many of them probably were quite illegal, not having been through the necessary process of registration and authorisation to make them "tolerated cults" (*religiones licitae*) in the eyes of the law, and naturally, since they were private, extant literature has next to nothing to say about them. Archaeology is rather more informative, and a number of monuments of one kind or another throw gleams of light upon the subject. One of the most famous is the Porta Maggiore basilica. Discovered by accident during the first World War, this subterranean building has the lines of a Romanesque Christian church, a basilica in the technical sense. It apparently never was used, for no traces have been found in it of ritual of any kind

[1] For the worship of Dionysos, see *Ancient Greek Religion*, p. 60 foll.

except a few bones under the floor which probably represent a foundation-sacrifice. Its walls are covered, especially those of the apse at that end where the altar would stand if it were a Christian church, with mythological scenes in stucco, some of them coloured, to which there is little doubt that an allegorical meaning was attached. For example, one handsome medallion shows the rape of Ganymede, and it is probable that this alludes to the carrying off of the soul, presumably to a higher life than that on earth. It is not unusual to speak of this strange monument as Pythagorean, but in the absence of any text or inscription, it is wisest not to be dogmatic. It seems to have been stripped in antiquity of all movable furnishings, and we may not be wrong in supposing that the sect, whatever it was, which used it was quickly suppressed as a *religio illicita* or unauthorised superstition. It was thought for a while that it might be connected with the unfortunate T. Statilius Taurus, who, according to Tacitus, was accused at Agrippina's instigation, chiefly of magical practices, and committed suicide in A.D. 53. No real evidence for this was forthcoming, but this much may be taken as certain, that the basilica was constructed for some congregation including persons of wealth and taste, who could command the services of skilled workmen and very tolerable artists to make their place of worship secluded and handsome. Another famous monument is at Pompeii, the celebrated Villa Item, on the outskirts of the town, on the walls of which are a great series of frescoes, again the subject of much discussion, but certainly connected with Dionysos and as certainly showing some of the rites of some kind of initiation. Much else has come to light in one part or another of the country, and amid all difficulties of interpretation, and after making liberal allowance for mythological or religious subjects being used by decorators merely as ornaments, it is clear that the religious life of Italy under the early Empire was lively. This does not mean that the traditional public cults, or their new fellows, the worships set up by the early Emperors, were neglected in favour of these less-known expressions. On the contrary, they seem to have been maintained with considerable zeal, especially those which pertained directly to the Imperial house. To be the *flamen* of Augustus, when he died and was officially deified, was no small distinction, and there were minor posts in connexion with the cult which give harmless play to the ambition of little men (not least of lower-class Italians) to have a title of some kind and a show of official duties to perform. These, however, were matters rather of tactful Governmental policy, to attach as many individuals as possible to the régime, than of religion properly so called. More to the point is the existence of a great number of little associations which had at least a flavour of religious sanction. These were quite legal ; a decree of the Senate laid down the maximum number of meetings they might hold and other matters, important to the general public policy of not allowing private organisations to be of any formidable size or power. They often described themselves as the "worshippers" (*cultores*) of this or that deity or little group of deities ; and they often were really nothing more than burial clubs, which collected a subscription from their members and in return undertook to give any one of them who died in good standing a respectable funeral, with the usual accompaniment of a funeral feast, often on a very modest scale. But that some of them were really little congregations of people who had some common religious interest is suggested by the fact that we have an inscription in rather halting verse put up by a *cultor Verbi*. In other words, we have some reason to suppose that an occasional group of Christians, in days before their religion had won its way to State recognition, disguised themselves under this inoffensive and legal form, substituting for the name of any recognised god, Roman or foreign, that of the divine Logos of the Fourth Gospel. If they did so, members of other unrecognised religions may have done the same.

At all events, be the organisation of these private cults what it may, there was a considerable and growing demand for a personal religion, and not least for one which should assure its adherents some hope of reward and advancement in another world, if not in this. The very feeling of helplessness in face of the great forces of the State and of Destiny led, as might be expected, to two results at least among the non-philosophical who could not find comfort in so rarified an atmosphere as that of Stoic speculations. One was a mere cynical indifference; life was of no great consequence, death ended it once and for all, therefore there was nothing about which anyone need concern himself very much. Tomb-inscriptions give evidence enough of this. There is a stock formula, occurring in both Greek and Latin, which runs: "I was not; I came to be; I am not; I care not". It is so familiar that Latin-using monumental masons often repre-sented it simply by the initial letters of the words. The other was the hope, doubtless vague in detail and unsupported by any reasoned scheme of eschatology, of some kind of con-tinued individual life after death, in which the liberated soul might enjoy the fellowship of superior beings. One very pretty example of this is probably to be found in the sarco-phagus and wall-painting commemorating a small child, Octavia Paulina, who died when seven years old and was buried in a vault belonging to her family. The former shows a little girl winning a wrestling match against a Cupid of the familiar childish type, often called an *amorino*. The latter is a kind of children's Elysion. A chariot is shown carrying, not Pluto with the ravished Persephone, but another *amorino* holding a small girl, and approaching an open place where a number of other children are playing around a statue of Hekate the infernal goddess. It is difficult, in this as in very many other cases, to determine how much is the result of serious belief and how much is mere pretty fancy on the part either of the child's parents or of the artist they em-ployed; but if the former be the case, we can parallel the pictures from literature. To die is often spoken of as a victorious achievement; the child on the sarcophagus is winning her wrestling-match. Mystic initiates, as we shall see in the next chapter, not infrequently pass through the experiences which their gods once had; little Octavia apparently is undergoing the same adventure as Persephone. It is quite possible that her parents belonged to some mystic sect and even that she herself had been through a ceremony of initiation, which was by no means confined to adults.

However, the best-known of these cults, which seem also

to have been the most influential and popular, were not of native Roman, or even of Greek origin, but came from farther east. It is therefore time to discuss the Oriental cults which made their way into the Roman world.

CHAPTER V

ORONTES INTO TIBER

IN a celebrated tirade against foreign elements in Rome, Juvenal uses the phrase which gives this chapter its title.

"Fellow-citizens," he says, "I cannot bear a Greek Rome ; and yet, what percentage of our slum-population is Greek ? Syrian Orontes flowed into the Tiber long ago and carried with it their language and their habits".

Oriental influence, indeed, was already old when he wrote these lines, early in the second century A.D. In 205 B.C., Hannibal was no longer a serious menace, but he was still holding a remote corner of Italy, and the people, strained by a desperate war which had lasted for twelve years, were but too ready to believe and fear every portent that was reported to them from any quarter. Showers of stones (doubtless volcanic lapilli) had occurred several times, and the Sibylline books were consulted. The response elicited from them was, according to Livy, to the effect that "when a foreign foe had invaded Italy, he could be driven out and vanquished if the Idaean Mother were brought from Pessinus". This was a Phrygian city, one of the most famous seats of a cult characteristic of Asia Minor and the neighbouring countries, that of the Great Mother. All over the Near East, though by no means confined to that part of the world, there was an early worship of a deity, varying in name and unessential attributes from place to place but always having one central characteristic ; she was fertile, the mother of all things that live on the earth, and often of the gods, or some of them, as well. Who her husband was, or if she had one, was a question not very important, and therefore producing no single consistent answer. At Pessinus, it was a minor deity, Attis, who was supposed to be her favourite, and concerning him an extraordinary tale was told. After sundry adventures connected with the goddess and her affection for him, he had castrated himself, and according to some accounts at least had died in consequence. His action was imitated by the priests of the goddess, the Galli, as the Greeks and Romans alike called them. The deity herself was commonly known as Kybelê or Kybêbê, and sometimes identified with the much less savage Greek Rhea. The object of this horrible rite of self-mutilation was probably in its origin an attempt to give the goddess more of the kind of *mana* she needed for her everlasting task of reproduction ; the severed parts were consecrated to her, while the Galli, if they survived, continued to be her ministers, but henceforth dressed like women. The Romans duly sent an embassy to the East, which went first to Delphoi to get Apollo's own assurance that the prophecy of his votary was true, then on to Asia, where, by the good offices of a friendly king, Attalos of Pergamon, they got possession of a shapeless black stone which "the natives said was the Mother of the Gods", Livy informs us, and brought it to Rome, where its arrival, at least according to legend, was heralded by a miracle, and its custody entrusted to a young member of the great family of the Scipios, who for reasons unknown to us was adjudged to be the best man in the whole State. The holy stone was temporarily lodged in the temple of Victory on the Palatine, where later a shrine was built for it and games, known as the Megalesia, or Festival of the Great (Mother), instituted in its honour.

Everything about the native cult of the goddess, especially the mutilation of the Galli and their outlandish dress and rites, was repugnant to Roman sentiment, therefore, having obeyed the divine command by receiving her, they took measures to keep her respectable and Roman, so far as was possible. The stone was set in the mouth of a decent statue of human form ; the priests were allowed occasionally to go about collecting contributions for their deity, but Romans were strictly forbidden to become Galli themselves. It would seem that the foreign priesthood, except for certain occasions, kept itself to the precincts of the temple ; these public appearances were, besides the begging expeditions, the annual ceremonial bath of the goddess, in the little river Anio, on March 27. But from an early date in the Empire (our evidence, such as it is, points to the principate of Claudius, A.D. 41-54), the old rules were relaxed. Roman names, though principally those of freedmen, appear in inscriptions among the priesthood, and the one day of the March festival was extended to five, with a preliminary observance on March 15th, the "entrance of the reeds", as its somewhat clumsy Latin title seems to have run. The cult-legend related this to Attis, who had been exposed when newly born and found by Kybelê in a reed-bed. The main ceremony, however, preceded by seven fast-days involving abstinence from bread, was the "entrance of the tree", a new-cut pine, carried by the Dendrophori or tree-bearers. Mystically, the tree was the dead Attis, and as such it was garlanded with violets and wrapped in linen. It is clear enough that the original Attis was one of those deities of vegetation who are born and die with the plants. The next day, spent in mourning and lamentation for the dead god, was followed by the wildest period of the whole rite, the Day of Blood, when the Galli lashed and cut themselves (presumably this was that familiar savage funeral rite, the offering of blood to the pale and bloodless dead) and their number was increased by the self-mutilations of novices whom fanaticism impelled to join their order. The following night, preceded by a period of strict fasting, was apparently spent in further laments for Attis, until, presumably early in the morning, the officiant proclaimed (in Greek verses, according to our informants ; no doubt the language of the cult had been Westernised to that extent) :

"Be of good cheer, initiates, seeing that the god is saved ; for we too, after our toils, shall find salvation".

Fasting and lamentations were now at an end, and the

next day, the Hilaria or Rejoicing, was spent in expressions of joy, apparently as wild as the mourning had been. It is no surprise that the Day of Rest followed ; and after it the original rite of the bathing of the goddess was carried out with all pomp and ostentation on the date which was that of the original shorter feast, March 27th.

It would be hard to imagine a performance more thoroughly unlike Roman ritual, or one fuller of morbid excitement. The date being fairly well on in the spring, something like a May Day would not be abnormal among any population which depended on the land for its sustenance ; dancing, merry-making, and a certain amount of general licence are the marks of such celebrations of the returning season of warmth and fertility, and associated with age-old ideas of the proper way to secure *mana* for the fields and for the flocks and herds. But the frenzy of the Great Mother's festival could scarcely be paralleled by anything European, ancient or modern, and that it should have been not only tolerated but popular in Rome shows clearly that the tone and sentiments of the population were changing. Juvenal was not far wrong when he implied that it was becoming an Oriental or at least a Greek city. The native Italian stock was perhaps diminishing, certainly not increasing much. The birth-rate among the higher classes was deplorably low, while the lower classes contained numbers of unemployed, or at best casual labourers, descendants of small farmers who had found conditions on the land impossible for them and so had betaken themselves to the doles and cheap amusements of the capital. Mixed with them was a great and increasing number of freedmen, who either had been slaves themselves or were the descendants of slaves, therefore were foreigners who could not care much for Roman traditions, while their own had been broken by exile and the often extremely degrading conditions of servitude. It is significant that by no means all were even Latin-speaking ; Greek inscriptions, put up by persons of freedman status and others, are common, and it is well known that the epistles both of St. Paul and St. Ignatius (martyred early in the second century A.D.) to the young Church of Rome are in

Greek. This miscellaneous rabble of nominal Romans, mixed with resident foreigners, had lost its last semblance of political power under Tiberius, when the elections of magistrates were transferred to the Senate in A.D. 14. It still, however, could be troublesome if it rioted, so the standing governmental policy was to keep it in good humour ; but little or nothing was done officially for its moral or educational improvement. It is therefore no wonder that non-Roman influences, good or bad, were rife.

One of these owed its beginnings to Sulla's campaigns in the Near East. His soldiers there came into contact with the goddess Ma (i.e. Mother) of Cappadocia, whose followers were even noisier than the Galli in their ritual. They were armed with swords and axes, with which, when wrought up into a frenzy by wild dancing attended by loud music, they cut themselves freely. They were supposed to be possessed by their goddess, and under that influence could prophecy ; as one of them foretold that Sulla would win against Marius, his great rival, he favoured the cult and let it be introduced into Rome, where it continued after his death in 78 B.C., and the "people of the shrine" (*fanatici*), as the Romans called them, were a familiar sight and sound in the City under the early Empire. The goddess herself was identified, owing presumably to the warlike appearance of her followers, with Bellona, the Roman war-goddess, associated with Mars, and so was commonly called by that name in Latin. She was, it would seem, no very formidable rival to the Great Mother, being indeed too much like her to constitute a counter-influence.

Kybelê's rites continued to increase in popularity, and were enlarged by two different kinds of ceremonial, the one savage and revolting, the other containing at least the germs of a lofty religion. The former, which can be traced back to the second century of our era, though its ultimate origins are obscure, was the notorious *taurobolium*. The word is Greek, like many of the technicalities of all these cults, for Greek, in forms more or less corrupt and degenerate, was the lingua franca of the Near East by that time, few of the native languages ever having more than a local popularity, for few of them had any literature at all, and a language not commonly written will not spread far beyond its native place. In Greece itself, none of these religions had much vogue.[1] *Taurobolium*, then, means properly the shooting of the bull (by means of arrows or other missiles), which indicates that the practice began somewhere in a district containing wild cattle. A bull was stood over a grating which covered a pit, and there killed with a hunting-spear. The person for whose benefit the rite was performed was in the pit, and received the blood from the slaughtered beast all over his body. He then emerged and the congregation bowed in veneration before him, for he was, as inscriptions assure us, "reborn for ever", although others, more modestly, limit the "new birth" to twenty years. In some cases a ram was substituted for the bull, but the effect was the same ; the man thus reborn was or became in either case a priest of the Great Mother, at least normally. It is fairly clear that the originators of the rite meant to acquire, by the blood of the sacred animal, perhaps an avatar of some god, something of his divine power and nature. The worshippers of Kybelê do not seem to have had so clear-cut a belief, though they held the ceremony to be very efficacious, and one of their most interesting inscriptions indicates that they somehow attached moral attributes to their savage performance, which they expressed in language derived ultimately from the Zoroastrian scriptures, the Gathas.

The other development was a comparatively spiritual and exalted cult of Attis. We have already seen that his worshippers were on occasion addressed as "initiates", and that they celebrated his death and resurrection with pious zeal. It will be remembered, also, that they were invited to base their own hopes of "salvation after their toils" upon the deliverance from death of their god. It would seem, therefore, that they were in some measure identified with him, a not uncommon phenomenon in cults, not so much of the classical world proper, as of those regions lying just east of it. The best-known form of the belief, which reached Greece at a fairly early date, perhaps the seventh century B.C., was that a worthy worshipper of Dionysos could gain, under

[1] See *Ancient Greek Religion*, p. 129.

certain circumstances, such identification with the god as to be called by his characteristic epithet, Bakchos. But it is likewise the central feature of the worships we are now discussing, which generally are known collectively as the mystery-cults. It seems likely that anyone who had undergone the *taurobolium* was "reborn", not as a human being but as Attis ; and apart from this unpleasing method of attaining permanent or temporary deity, we have a fragment of the ritual of a more sober cult. One of the Christian controversialists to whom we owe not a little knowledge of the later forms of paganism, Firmicus Maternus, who preached against what had once been his own religion or one like it with all the zeal of a convert, says in his interesting tract, *On the Error of Profane* (i.e., non-Christian) *Cults*, that the pagans had certain passwords, the result of "the devil's teaching", and that one of them, which he gives both in the original Greek and in a free Latin translation, ran :

I have eaten from the timbrel ; I have drunk from the cymbal ; I am become an initiate of Attis.

He then proceeds to thunder against it with all the force of his rhetorical powers and explain how much better is the Christian Eucharist. To those who look at such things calmly, away from the atmosphere of religious controversies now long dead, it is an interesting formula, for it bears a resemblance which can hardly be accidental to one adduced by St. Clement of Alexandria as belonging to the Eleusinian Mysteries.

I fasted ; I drank the *kykeon ;* I took from the sacred chest ; I wrought therewith and put it in the basket, and from the basket into the chest.

The *kykeon* was a ritual drink containing water, meal and some other ingredients. Clement also knows a fuller version of the formula concerning Attis, in which the initiate mentions two more sacral actions, carrying a vessel called a *kernos*, of very ancient fashion and used in other mystic rites as well, and entrance into the *pastos* or marriage-chamber. Naturally, these formulae are not explicit ; they do not, for instance, tell us what the Eleusinian initiate took from the chest nor what he "wrought" with it, nor why the votary of Attis carried the *kernos*, what the marriage-chamber was nor what he did in it. His co-religionists would know, and the profane were meant to be left uninformed. But from what we know or can guess concerning rites of this kind, we are left with some information. The devotee of Attis ate and drank from sacred utensils, musical instruments of oriental types used in the service of their deity. He thus partook of a sacred feast, the food and drink being charged with the holiness of the god. At some time during the ritual, whether the occasion to which the password refers or not, the initiate drank milk, and as that is the food of babies, it was interpreted by some at least as a symbol of rebirth. There exists a late but interesting treatise by one Sallustius, probably that Sallustius who was a friend of Julian the Apostate, Emperor 361-363 A.D. and would-be restorer of paganism, which explains it so, and furthermore, finds in the whole series of rites, from the cutting of the pine-tree onwards (see above, p. 126), a deep allegory of the return of the human soul from its present unworthy environment to the company of the gods whence it sprang. Sallustius is far from being an original thinker, and it may be taken as certain that his interpretations were those of many pious followers of this or similar religions. Thus we find that out of a cult originally grotesque, revolting and founded upon notions belonging to a barbarous stage of human development, there could arise, with the admixture of a little Greek philosophy, a faith anything but degraded, though hampered with the need for explaining away many features of ritual which no Westerner would welcome save under the influence of a conviction that in these barbarian practices there lurked ancient wisdom and a system both metaphysical and ethical which was worthy of admiration and adoption.

The spiritual adventurer of Roman Imperial days was not confined to the cult of Attis in his search for a personal religion to satisfy his aspirations. The Egyptian cults had taken a new and less markedly national form under the Macedonian dynasty of the Ptolemies, and had spread from

Egypt into parts of the Greek world, and thence to Italy. Like Attis, the gods of the Nile had adopted Greek as their means of communication with foreigners, though deep veneration for the ancient and mysterious-looking cult of their native land was certainly one of the influences which made for their success. Osiris, whatever he may originally have been, had certainly become by the time of which I am now speaking a dying and rising god, in that respect like Attis and also like the Thraco-Phrygian Dionysos, with whom indeed he was often. identified, though perhaps not for that reason. The Egyptian legend, probably not much distorted from its native form, although Greek influence is patent here and there, was well known to Plutarch, who is indeed our chief authority for it. He omits, as he plainly tells us, certain "superfluous and needless" details, and the rest is, in outline, as follows. Osiris, Isis and Typhon (Set, a very ancient Egyptian god whose cult had given place to that of Osiris, with the result that Set was represented as desperately wicked) were three of the five children born at one time of Rhea, i.e., the native goddess Netpe. Osiris and Isis, lovers from the very beginning, became husband and wife, and Osiris rose speedily to be a beneficent and mighty king. But Typhon was frantically jealous of him, and by a trick persuaded him to lie down in a coffin which exactly fitted his body (as an Egyptian mummy-case would). He and his confederates immediately put on the lid, made it fast and threw the coffin into one of the mouths of the Nile. Isis, in wild grief, searched for her husband and at length found the coffined body, which so far revived that Isis had a son by it ; she already had one child, the god Horos. Typhon and his confederates, however, were still on the watch, and this time stole the body, cut it into fourteen pieces and cast it into various places, whence Isis, slowly and with infinite pains, recovered nearly all. She then trained her son to be a formidable avenger of his father, and when grown he fought and defeated Typhon, whom, however, Isis would not put to death, to Horos' great wrath.

Osiris, among a people with so lively a belief in a corporeal and material survival of death as the Egyptians, naturally enough became a ruler of the dead, since his body had at last been rescued, but he was something more than that, even in Egyptian belief pure and simple. For historical and other reasons, there was a great tendency in that country to identify different gods and ascribe attributes to one which originally had belonged to another ; a phenomenon which appears also in Graeco-Roman religion and is known to moderns by the clumsy name of syncretism. It need not therefore surprise anyone that Osiris tends now and again to be confused with Rê, the great sun-god, to the extent at least of having some solar traits himself, and also with the god of the Nile. In these capacities he is not a god of the dead, at least not of them alone, but of the living. Certainly he was concerned with living men in the form his cult assumed abroad. Egypt also had celebrated rites which, to a Greek, suggested his own mysteries, at Eleusis or elsewhere, in which mourning for the loss of Osiris was followed, it would seem, by re-joicing at his recovery. These accompanied him, in forms which may very well have been modified and elaborated on the way, into the Greek-speaking and thence into the Roman world.

However, the gracious figure of Isis, the divine wife and mother, was still more striking and popular. The various mother-goddesses already existing were less formidable rivals to her than might have been expected, for the same tendency to syncretism enabled her to be simply identified with them. In the *Golden Ass*, to which we shall refer shortly, she appears to the hero and tells him that she is called the Mother of the Gods in Phrygia, Athena in Athens, Aphrodite in Cyprus, and so forth, but Isis is her real name and the Egyptians know her own rites. What was unedifying or grotesque in her legend was explained away by allegories, or simply omitted, and she was exalted in the belief of many thousands as a deity full of grace and of power to help in this world and the next, with whom were associated a number of doctrines often vague and fantastic, but not degrading. Especially, it would seem, resident foreigners in Italy and the poorer classes generally were fascinated by her, though her worshippers were by no means confined to the lower ranks. In her cult, something new to the west was introduced. As already mentioned, a Roman god, or for that matter a Greek one, had nothing corresponding to the daily and hourly ritual of the more elaborate Christian ceremonials. Isis had ; and the fact that her clergy had their continual round of duties in her service must have impressed those who saw them with the idea of a *numen* ever present and ready and willing to listen. She and her attendant deities, Osiris himself, Anubis, Horos and the Ptolemaic Graeco-Egyptian god Sarapis were something new and exciting, which as long as the Egyptian shrine was present in Rome was at the very doors of the faithful. Governmental opposition was in vain. The Egyptian gods' chapels were torn down four times in ten years (between 58 and 48 B.C.), but they always rose again, and at last, in 43 B.C., the provisional government which immediately succeeded Julius Caesar thought of building a temple at public expense. This was not done, and shortly afterwards the rivalry between Octavian and Antony which culminated in the Battle of Actium and the capture of Alexandria, Antony's capital (31 and 30 B.C.) made everything connected with Alexandria and Egypt unpopular. But the goddess was not to be denied ; repeated prohibitions of her worship within Rome, or at least within the sacred *pomerium*, were evaded, and at last the half-mad Caligula, in or about A.D. 38, put up a temple to her in the Campus Martius, practically in Rome though sacrally outside it. This one of his acts remained unchallenged ; the various scandals aimed at the Egyptian priesthood died down and Isis and her retinue enjoyed Imperial favour thenceforth.

We are in a position to estimate what her cult meant to a pious, or rather pietistic, mind, that of the rhetorician, mystic and perhaps dabbler in magic, Apuleius of Madaura in Africa (second century A.D.). We have from him a brilliantly written romance, the *Metamorphoses*, otherwise known as the *Golden Ass*. His plot, which is Greek and probably a folk-tale originally, tells of a young man, by name Lucius, who by mishandling a charm turns himself into an ass and can resume his human shape only by eating fresh roses. In his attempts to get this remedy, he passes through a long series of grotesque and not always edifying adventures, told with great verve and in a rich, though intensely artificial style. At last Isis appears to him, tells him to snatch a rose-garland from her priest at her spring festival, claims his devotion and promises her protection in this world and the other. He follows her directions, and in due course is initiated into her mysteries. Apuleius cannot, naturally, divulge any details of what he (for there is little doubt that at this point he is describing his own experiences) went through, but his hints are enough to be interesting. He approached, he tells us, the bounds of Death and trod on the threshold of Proserpina, returning thence through all the four elements. He saw the sun at midnight, drew near the gods of the lower and the upper worlds and worshipped them face to face. In the morning, he was exhibited to an adoring congregation in the full dress of a sun-god. Later he passed through two more initiations and became one of the minor clergy, of an order which had its seat in Rome and claimed to have been founded in the days of Sulla.

We thus see that the Egyptian deities had to offer (though, as Apuleius clearly indicates, not at cheap rates) a most impressive ritual, well calculated to stir intense feelings in those who underwent it, and leading, in the case of the more devout, to something not unlike a monastic life. For those who felt no such vocation, there were lesser degrees of intimacy with the deities, down to mere occasional attendance at the temple-services, which indeed it was said by ill-wishers were made excuses for more earthly pleasures, in the shape of assignations of lovers. Juvenal has no better epithet than "procuress" for Isis, and a very bad scandal in the days of Tiberius led to one of the periodical suppressions of the cult and the crucifixion of the priests in A.D. 19. How much of all this was mere gossip, such as naturally forms around a foreign cult kept partly secret, and how much was founded on fact, it would be idle to ask now. For those philosophically inclined, explanations of the legends and rites were abundant, and might lead them into all manner of interesting and trans-cendental speculations, of a kind then popular. For all alike, it was a personal and moving religion, dependent neither on the formalities of State cult nor on the mere vagaries of private piety, and it had also, what counted then for a great deal, the prestige of an immemorial antiquity. Ancient civilisation had by that time lost the fresh self-confidence of its earlier days, and reverence for the supposed deep and mysterious wisdom of those who had lived long ago, especially in foreign lands, was common. These men were nearer the gods, and therefore more likely to know the truth concerning them, and from their teaching had sprung all that was best in Greek theology. No life of a philosopher, save those of the more materialistic schools, such as Epicurus, was complete without an account of how he went abroad, generally to Egypt, to learn wisdom from the native priests. Here and there such stories have some foundation in fact ; for example, there is evidence that Plato was interested in both Persian and Egyptian ideas ; but the exaggeration in most of them is gross, and some are doubtless pure fiction. One very quaint outcome of this craze for ancient and foreign revelations has proved acceptable to modern researchers. The Christians shared it, and were interested to prove that the Hebrew religion was the oldest in the world. In this attempt, they studied the Greek chronologers with great diligence, and so it comes about that much of our knowledge of indispensable dates for ancient history is derived from material preserved by controversialists such as St. Cyril of Alexandria, Eusebios the ecclesiastical historian and his translator and supplementer, St. Jerome. The results at which these men arrived for the earlier periods are of course grotesquely wrong, but the data they preserve are often of high value, for the computations of ancient scholars, especially the Alexandrians, were often exact for fully historical times, not far wrong even as far back as the eighth century B.C., and not seldom suggestive for events more remote than that. Their great weakness, that they knew little of archaeology and nothing of scientific methods of excavation, has been supplied in modern times.

The cults with which we have been dealing attracted all classes and professions ; we have now to expound one which was largely military. The god Mithra (Mithras in Greek) had long been worshipped in Iran, a region whose influence was widespread and felt in the West, for after the overthrow of the Persian monarchy by Alexander the Great, there was a political revival, culminating in the establishment of powerful dynasties, first foreign and later native, in Persia and the neighbouring countries, while the cultural exports never stopped. Zarathustra, the Zoroaster of Graeco-Roman tradition, had founded a lofty religion in his native country, which, mingled with elements often quite foreign to his ideas and principles, spread in all directions, resulting in cults so different from each other as modern Parsism in India and the mysteries of Mithra in the Roman Empire. The fundamental aspect of his teaching was its dualism ; the universe, to him, is the seat of a long-drawn war between the powers of good and evil, whereof the latter, though destined to ultimate defeat, is so strong as to make the contest a real one in which the forces of good readily welcome human aid. Zoroastrians, therefore, formed a veritable church militant, and it is thus not surprising that Mithraism, the most famous and popular development of the Persian religion in the West, appealed especially to regular soldiers. They were not, indeed, Mithra's first votaries in Italy. According to a much quoted passage of Plutarch, in his life of Pompey, the pirates whom that general suppressed, though ruthless in their desecration of other people's shrines, had a religion of their own, centring about Olympos (one of the two mountains of that name in Asia Minor, not the traditional seat of the Greek gods), where they performed certain strange sacrifices and secret rites, whereof those of Mithras survive to this day and were taught by them.

Pompey, who was inclined towards mercy when it was politic, spared many of the pirates when they surrendered to him, and settled them in Italy, where Vergil afterwards knew one of them, quite reformed and an enthusiastic and skilled market-gardener. But it would seem that they brought their gods with them, and that from this rather unpromising source the religion spread. However, there were plenty of other opportunities for Roman armies to become acquainted with Persian or partly Persian rites and doctrines during their many campaigns in the Near East, and we need not suppose that the pirates were the only missionaries.

There were at least three features in the new cult which made it attractive to a variety of minds. In the first place, like all dualistic systems, Zoroastrianism and its offshoots offered a solution of the existence of evil in a world the rightful ruler of which is a good and wise God. Plainly, if there is another power, almost as strong as and diametrically opposed to the good deity, which continually wars against his sovranty, it is no wonder that evil should often meet with some measure of success, bringing, for example, plague and famine on innocent populations. Not a few philosophers, from the time of Plato onwards, thought such a doctrine worthy of serious examination. In the particular case of Mithra, there was another dogma attractive to some philosophers at least, those of the more transcendental schools. Their idea of deity was so exalted that they had difficulty in reconciling his infinite greatness and purity with any sort of contact with the low and material affairs of mankind, and the need of some kind of intermediary was widely felt. "Mediary" (*mesites*) is precisely what Plutarch, in another passage, styles Mithra. Here, then, was a venerable revealed doctrine ready to confirm theories of the existence of beings less than fully divine but much superior to mankind which were already current. Next, and this is not unimportant for that age, Mithraism seems to have had a fairly developed moral code of its own ; at all events, Zoroastrianism had, and the emperor Julian knows of "commandments" (*entolai ;* it is the very word which, while still Christian, he would have used of the Decalogue), given by Mithra to his followers. After several centuries of moralising philosophy, many forms of which had been popularised and were known in outline to all and sundry by writings and lectures, a religion which paid no attention to ethics would have had little chance of wide acceptance. The State cults, which remained almost entirely matters of ceremonial, were for most people no more than a part of the decent formalities of life, especially public life. In the third place, Mithraism had a strict discipline and a hierarchic series of grades which seem to have made it especially attractive to soldiers. Mithra himself, in the East, had often been the patron of warlike kings, and some part of the technical language of his cult had a military flavour ; one of the grades of initiation was that of Soldier (*miles*).

From a number of fragmentary sources, written and un-written, it has been possible to patch together something like an outline picture of Mithraism, though the gaps in our knowledge are very many, no Mithraic treatise having sur-vived, if indeed any such were ever written, and much of our information coming either from opponents of this and all non-Christian cults, or else from sacred carvings and emblems easily understood by initiates, but never meant to be intelligible to outsiders. So far, then, as we can under-stand it, Mithraism had its sacred legend, as indeed all cults had, and according to this, Mithra was miraculously born from a rock, and after various episodes caught and tamed a huge bull, obviously a supernatural creature. This beast he afterwards sacrificed. This act is the central thing in Mithra-ism, and occupies at least as prominent a station in the decorations of their places of worship as the Crucifixion does in Christian art. We know, partly from Oriental sources, partly from the many surviving representations of the scene, that from the bull there sprang the plants and animals useful to mankind, although the emissaries of Ahriman, the evil power, tried to prevent this happy result. Mithra also entered into relations with the Sun-god, is shown feasting with him and riding in his chariot, and indeed is himself often identified with him, one of his commonest titles in dedications being *Sol inuictus*, the Unconquerable Sun. As such, his birthday is at the time of year when the sun, passing the winter solstice, begins to move towards his summer position and consequently to lengthen the days in the northern hemisphere. This was fixed at December 25th, hence the traditional date of Christ-mas is of Mithraic, not Christian origin. This is but one of several indications of a certain influence of the rival cults on one another ; it is possibly a borrowing in the other direction which lies behind a common scene of the adoration of the young god by shepherds.

Those who wished to devote themselves to the service of

Mithra entered upon a complicated series of initiations, seven in all, the names of which are preserved for us by St. Jerome, with some doubt as to one of them, which seems to have been miscopied, and no certainty that he has them in the right order, for he mentions them only in passing, while speaking of the destruction of a Mithraic sanctuary by a fanatical Christian official. They are, including the doubtful name, Raven, Hidden one (?), Soldier, Lion, Persian, Sun-runner (Heliodromus) and Father. The holders of all these grades were men, women having no part or only a subordinate one in this religion. The initiations comprised sundry tests of the neophyte's courage and determination, remnants likely enough of older rites of a more savage kind, and it may have been purely a matter of choice how high in the order anyone tried to rise. How it was determined that the holder of a lower grade might be allowed to proceed to a higher one, we do not know.

Mithra himself was a righteous god, as befitted one of the allies of Ahura Mazda, the Zoroastrian deity. He was "holy" (*sanctus*) according to many mentions of him on inscriptions. He loved the truth and hated lies, for lies are of Ahriman. His followers were comrades, presumably with mutual duties. The ideal of purity which was an essential part of all Persian religion seems to have been no merely ceremonial affair for them, but to have had its moral side as well. We may safely take it that the faithful follower of this Persian god led a clean life and, at least towards his co-religionists, one of honour and honesty. His reward was to be in the life to come, and here the Zoroastrian ideas of the ultimate salvation of the good when the wicked, along with Ahriman himself, are consumed by the fire which shall end the age, were modified by astrological doctrines with which Zarathustra himself never had anything to do. Astrology taught that the human soul, on its way to earth, passed through the spheres of the seven planets, and from each of them got the appropriate passion, lust for instance in the sphere of Venus, anger in that of Mars and so on. Indeed, it has been plausibly maintained that the canonical list of the seven deadly sins is astrological and pre-Christian in its origin. Whether this is so or not, it would seem that the seven Mithraic grades correspond to the seven planetary spheres, and that the finally delivered soul, protected by the god from the assaults of the evil powers, would rise through these spheres, losing at each one of the passions which had troubled him on earth, to a realm of perfect light and purity. This last idea, that the souls of the good go literally to heaven, was not peculiar to Mithraism, but common to several faiths of that time ; we see it in Christianity, in one of the most misunderstood passages of the Apocalypse, where the spirits of the martyrs are "under the Altar", meaning the constellation of that name, which in Mediterranean latitudes is always low on the horizon. They are newly dead, and so have just arrived on the borders of the sky. But it is very much older than St. John the Theologian. A kind of forerunner of it appears as early as Aristophanes, who mentions a belief that stars are souls of the dead. But the coming of astrological belief brought a much more elaborate form of it, somewhat as sketched above, while before that, the doctrine, common to several schools of philosophical and semi-philosophical thought, that the human soul is of divine origin and may in time ascend to the place whence it came, led to the natural corollary, that the just ascend to the presence of the gods, or at least to some lower region of their dwelling-place, such as the moon, conceived as the dividing-mark between the imperfect world in which we live and that in which, owing to the absence of dense and stubborn matter such as earth and water, the immutable laws of the universe are perfectly obeyed.

Much more might be said, did the dimensions of this book permit it, of other cults which came in from the East or contained Oriental elements and found their followers in the Graeco-Roman world of the Empire. But what has been said may serve to mark their characteristic features,—a central doctrine of a god friendly to man, often a suffering god (Mithra, to judge by his expression in many works of art, sacrificed his bull only at great violence to his feelings), in many cases one who dies and rises again ; a process of initiation, often elaborate and long-drawn-out ; and a code which included moral as well as ceremonial precepts. In all alike, personal salvation and happiness after death were assured to the faithful ; in all alike, the deity worshipped had strongly astral connexions, identification of all manner of important figures, not Mithra only, with the Sun being extremely common.

It is thus evident that when Christianity became widely known and was no longer conceived by the average person to be merely a new and disreputable variety of Judaism, it found the ground well prepared for it. Even its Scriptures, the Greek versions of the Old Testament, though not much read (well-informed writers like Tacitus and Strabo show complete ignorance of them), still had spread beyond the Jewish nation, for Judaism was then an actively propagandising religion, and converts and enquirers were numerous. As soon as they were known, they won attention. Here were documents professing to go back to the very beginning of human history, to be direct revelations and to contain forecasts of events which afterwards took place. Moreover, they agreed in many places with the deeply respected prophecies of the Sibyls (cf. p. 94) ; for the critical powers of that age were seldom developed enough for it to be suspected, what is now very evident, that the Sibylline verses generally current were blatant forgeries, drawing for much of their material on the Jewish documents themselves. If understood according to schools of allegorical interpretation which had established themselves in the Greek-using world since about the beginning of our era, the Scriptures contained in a more authoritative form the teachings of some of the most popular philosophies, notably the current developments of Platonism. They preached, along with a complicated ceremonial code, a lofty morality and a monotheistic theology. Even the extraordinary foreigner's Greek in which they were expressed was no great handicap, for it was little if at all worse than what many of the new hearers used themselves, and many of the oddest phrases had the attraction of sounding very mysterious. Now came a set of new teachers, who proclaimed with the utmost courage and zeal, despite all the handicaps under which an unauthorised cult laboured, and despite occasional local outbursts of savage repression, that the predictions in these venerable documents had been fulfilled in a Person born so recently that he could be dated by reference to figures familiar to everyone, such as Augustus, whose life-story was encumbered by no unedifying or fantastic legends, whose doctrine was of the purest and loftiest, and whose death was declared to have been followed by a triumphant resurrection, quite after the approved pattern, while his return in the full glory of divinity was almost hourly expected. About the new doctrine there soon gathered a ritual elaborate enough to be impressive, but again marked by no repulsive features, and containing the essential element of initiation into mysteries, namely those ceremonies, especially the Eucharist, which were not for outsiders, and to which catechumens were admitted only after sufficient instruction in the articles of their new faith. Here again was a strong point, which the young Church shared only with Judaism ; regular instruction was to be had, and as time went on, those intellectually inclined could receive more and more elaborate philosophical teaching, of good enough quality to attract some of the best minds of the early Christian centuries. If we may judge by what is left of the arguments on the other side, the Christian apologists, with all their faults, were neither so credulous nor such bad logicians as their opponents. For the less intellectual, there was a feeling of comradeship in a great adventure. To adopt Christianity was always more or less dangerous until the acceptance of it as a State religion by Constantine. Those who died for their faith did so in the fervent hope that they should be richly rewarded in a future life, while in the meantime all were assured of the support of a growing community which not only recognised in theory the equality of its members with each other but outstripped all other religious bodies in the practical generosity with which it dealt with its poor. That the new religion was of Eastern origin was in that age no handicap, but rather the reverse. The asceticism which grew up within it during the first few centuries of its existence was nothing new or peculiar, but was shared with several other cults of longer standing.

Since there were many points of contact, both in ethics

and in metaphysics, with other religions, it is not remarkable that several mixed systems grew up, classified by the Christian writers as heresies and often marked by most fantastic doctrines, formed of elements from very diverse sources. Doubtless there were many more compromises of which we hear nothing. The story told of the emperor Alexander Severus, that his private chapel contained figures of Orpheus, Abraham and Christ, may not be true, but there is nothing in it essentially incredible. Such phenomena as the appearance of Orpheus in Christian art and of Christian names in pagan magic are indicative of the broad-minded readiness of many to take and use anything that attracted them in any of the miscellaneous systems then available. It will be seen that the most popular, Christian and pagan, had in common several features, namely a doctrine of something like redemption through the efforts of a supernatural being, a moral code, a ritual, and a hope of blessedness in a future state. Hence, although conversions were normally from paganism, or Judaism, to Christianity, quite genuine conversions also from Christianity to paganism in one of its more refined and philosophic forms were not unheard of ; the case of the emperor Julian was the most celebrated, not the only one. No importance, of course, attaches either to the frequent apostacies from Christianity during the persecutions or to the general movement towards it when it was assured of Imperial support ; such things are unheroic but human and natural reactions.

One class of the population, however, was reluctant to give up its old traditional practices under the influence either of Christianity or of the other foreign religions. The country people went on much as before with their ancestral ways of getting the *numen* they wanted for their fields and their beasts. A reflexion of this is seen in the shift of meaning of the word *paganus* itself. Originally it was soldiers' slang, about equivalent to "civvy", meaning one who stays at home in his village (*pagus*) and does not join the forces. Hence it came to mean one who was not a soldier of Christ, not a member of the Church militant. But more than one of the fathers implies that to them the word means "rustic", rather one who is too stupid to see the truth of Christianity than too timid or unenterprising to join it. This attitude lasted in the countryside after the opposition in the cities, centering around the sentimental and antiquarian revival of paganism in Rome itself during the last generation or two before its official extinction, had collapsed before governmental edicts. It was part of the politic and tactful wisdom of the Christian clergy that they did not merely destroy but replaced in the country districts, giving the farmers, for instance, a substitute for the vanished Ambarualia (see p. 35) in the blessing of the fields with the Litania Maior, while ancient local holinesses were kept everywhere under new names, wells for example all over the civilised world becoming the wells of saints instead of local godlings and losing none of their reputation for healing and other good powers in the process. A little remains to be said of such substitutions in the final chapter.

CHAPTER VI

SURVIVALS

IF anyone set out to write a history of the survivals of Graeco-Roman cult in the Western world, the "remaines of Gentilisme" as John Audrey called them in 1686/87, he would find himself committed to a long and learned treatise involving a wide review of European folklore from the date of that edict of Theodosius (A.D. 392), which formally prohibited all forms even of private pagan cult, down to the present day. Furthermore, he would be obliged to examine in detail many features of the history of the declining Empire itself, and unravel the complicated story of how the cult of deified Emperors and of the Genius of the living one passed in time into a theocracy in which the ruling monarch was treated as already divine, and from that into an absolutism in which the sovrans were official defenders of the Faith (or, as occasionally happened, of the prevailing heresy of the time) and still ruled by divine right. He would have to pass under observation isolated struggles between the old ways and the new, such as the occasional killing of a too zealous cleric who tried to interfere with the rites of some remote country district, the slow disappearance of the old festivals from the calendars and from popular memory, or the conversion of surviving temples into Christian holy places (Apollo did not finally yield his hold on Monte Cassino, for instance, till St. Benedict put up his monastery there in 529). He would have to consider at length the extent to which the very names survived ; there is, for instance, reason to take San Miniato at Florence as being originally nothing more than the Holy One painted with *minium*, the traditional red pigment with which Etruscan and Roman statues of gods (in this case perhaps Juppiter, or his Etruscan equivalent Tinia) were daubed. He would find abundant room for the exercise of his judgment on the question to what extent this or that prominent man of the later times was anything more than a purely nominal Christian ; Ausonius of Bordeaux, in his day a writer of great popularity, who enjoyed favour and preferment under the emperor Gratian (murdered A.D. 383), is a case in point. Certainly he was no fanatic for any kind of religion, and was puzzled and distressed when his friend Paulinus of Nola embarked upon the pious courses which led in time to his canonisation. He would need to study the lives of missionary saints and other Christian worthies, trying to discover whether, when they are said to have replaced this or that Roman cult by their own faith, they were really doing so or attacking some native Gaulish, German or other deity, roughly identified with a familiar mythological figure. The whole question of the transit from serious belief in stories of the traditional gods to half- or quarter-belief in what ancient theorists called "poets' theology" and from that again to literary ornament so harmless that no one any longer objected to it, would occupy him at some length. He would give much attention to the question to what extent the more popular saints are, as has been epigrammatically said, "successors of the gods", and, even before that, to the very vexed question of the amount of influence exercised upon Christianity itself by the various mystery-religions which, as we have seen, were its competitors and to a great extent prepared the way for it. The ecclesiastical calendar would force itself upon his attention, with its many dates reminiscent of pre-Christian festivals—St. Joseph, for instance, occupying the date of the Quinquatrus (see p. 64), March 19th, while the Annunciation supplies the place of the Hilaria (p. 127), St. Mark that of the Robigalia (p. 73) on April 25th, St. Cyprian replaces Juppiter on September 13th, and so forth, raising for each date the problem whether we have to do with replacement or mere coincidence. Obviously, nothing of this kind can even be attempted in the concluding pages of a short outline ; it seems, therefore, better to take a single example, the development of a late ancient festival into that modern one which is most universally popular, Christmas.

Two very ancient themes unite in this festival. One is the importance of all beginnings, and consequently of the beginning of the year. Now the solar year may begin naturally at any one of four points, the two solstices and the two equinoxes, and all four have been used by one community or another at various times. The Roman calendar, as reformed by Caesar, began where ours does, with January 1st, which of course is not a solstice now and was not in his day, but is fairly near it, too near for any lengthening of the daylight to be perceptible. The other is the widespread tendency to set the powers of cold and darkness at defiance just when they are at their most formidable, in the dark days of mid-winter, the northern Yule. In Europe, this is also a season when, in the old rustic economy at least, food is abundant for the time being, especially in the north, when there was not until fairly recently enough winter fodder for all the cattle, and so a number of them were slaughtered late in the autumn and their flesh salted down or consumed on the spot. It is thus a season when it is possible to feast and make merry, and the impossibility of doing much farm-work, owing to the state of the weather, gives further opportunity for a holiday. At this time of year, then, Rome had a series of popular holidays, the Saturnalia of December 17th (p. 77), the Compitalia of January (p. 38), and, newest of all, New Year's Day, the Kalends of January. Under the early Empire, this was not yet a great holiday, but had its observances, because it was a beginning. Presents (*strenae*, French *étrennes*) were interchanged ; they seem to have been of trifling value, consisting of sweet things, such as honey, and small coins, the equivalents in symbols of the good wishes which were interchanged, for clearly they express a hope (or even may be taken as a charm) that the year may be both pleasant and profitable to the recipient. Courts of law were closed, the new magistrates formally entered upon their office with the usual sacrifices to Juppiter on the Capitol, and everyone performed some small piece of his usual work, no doubt something which he could finish quickly and well, in hopes that everything he did at his occupation might likewise be done easily and thoroughly during the next twelve months. It was, then, a festival partly at least official, certainly encouraged by governmental recognition, which extended to elaborate developments of the *strenae*, originally not even the simple presents which the early Empire knew, but merely twigs, probably to be used for the decoration of the house which was a feature of this and of all manner of other feasts. As the Empire went on, they became more and more expensive, included presents of great value to the Emperor and still more valuable ones made by him in return, and finally became such a burden that the emperors Arcadius and Honorius limited their amount in A.D. 395 and Leo abolished them in 458, so far at least as the loyal offerings were concerned ; what subjects chose to give each other remained their own concern, as before. By that time, these gifts were connected, not with New Year's Day proper, but with January 3rd, the day on which it had been the custom to make formal vows for the welfare of the Emperor, hence the name Vota which it commonly bore.

So far as the general public was concerned, the festival had but small beginnings. The first of every month was a festival from very ancient times, hence no one objected to celebrating January 1st ; but it had not even been officially the beginning of the year till 153 B.C., and had no particular hold on popular affections. However, as it was the greatest official day of that season, and as it fell but a fortnight after the widely popular Saturnalia, naturally enough usages belonging to that festival came little by little to be transferred to it. The Compitalia likewise contributed to it, since it lay between the two ancient feasts ; this would give it country support also, for with the passing of the richer classes especially to the city, turning over the actual care of their estates to slaves or free subordinates, the Saturnalia had became more the feast of town-dwellers and their households there, the Compitalia the winter holiday of farm-workers. Gradually the Kalends, now a festival several days long and leading up to the Ludi Compitales of January 3rd-5th, became perhaps the greatest holiday time of the whole year, when everyone feasted, made merry, gave and received gifts, and incidentally, as before, sought for favourable omens. It was thundered against by a succession of Fathers of the Church and numerous Councils, but with very little effect either on its merriment or its superstitions. Popular astrology, with its doctrine that the destiny of anything, including the business of a year, could be foretold by consulting the stars at the beginning of it, had got its hold on the people before the Church was ready, and to put down any popular festival is generally possible only by substituting another for it. We shall see that gradually this was done for part of Western and Northern Europe.

But the Roman Empire was a very extensive territory with a most miscellaneous population, and the Roman customs, as they spread, met and mingled with all manner of foreign rites. In the East, the winter festival season was crossed with sundry local customs, some very old. The most notorious of these was a descendant of the Babylonian Sakaia at which there was chosen, not the harmless "chief of the Saturnalia" (p. 77), but a mock-king who, after a brief period of unrestrained honours and pleasures, was put to death, and there is evidence that this was actually done, at least occasionally and among some units of the army, in Roman garrisons in the East. Another was the custom, also, it would seem, tolerated rather among soldiers than civilians, of going about in disguise, making broad fun of all manner of people, including the most respectable and highly placed. In the Keltic and Germanic regions of the West, another disguisement was met with ; here the mummers went about dressed as various kinds of beasts, probably a remnant of some seasonal festival of native gods, Gaulish or other, for in Gaul at all events gods often were represented under forms other than human. Thus custom after custom, Roman and foreign, accumulated in various parts of the Empire upon what had once been no more than a rather accentuated celebration of the first day of an officially important month. The Church authorities were extremely disgusted, but their attempts to make January 1st into a fast-day or at least a sober Christian holiday met with but poor success. To this day, January 1st is a time of considerable popularity in the Mediterranean regions, and not least in Greece, where, somewhat Christianised as the feast of St. Basil, it continues to be a time of traditional merry-makings and amusements, accompanied by good wishes and well-omened actions to introduce the New Year.

But the East, despite invasions and other political upsets, remained the most cultured part of the disintegrating Empire. In particular, it never became illiterate nor unable to use so civilised a thing as a calendar, with its astronomical basis and its computation of a series of days, calculated in an orderly manner from a fixed point and beginning again as soon as that point is once more reached. It was very different with the barbarous peoples who flooded the West. No such notion as a regular solar calendar had as yet entered their heads. They did indeed pick up from the Gauls, who had taken very kindly to Roman culture, some notion of the planetary week, and had gone so far as to find equivalents among their own gods for Juppiter, Venus and so forth, which still survive in the English, German and Scandinavian names for the week-days. They had in their own language sundry words vaguely denoting seasons, such as summer and winter, which are things anyone can perceive for himself and not periods consisting of a given number of days each. But a regular year, and therefore a New Year's Day, was strange and even meaningless to them, and was not likely to be made popular by the ecclesiastical objections to the New Year celebrations, for what culture and learning the new-comers got was, as is well known, conveyed to them from the same source which gave them such tincture of Christianity as they could, slowly and with many difficulties, be persuaded to accept. But, although they had no regular year, they had certain festivals, fixed approximately though not exactly, from which they might reckon, and one of these was the feast whose name in its English form is Yule. This was not a day but a period, and came in winter, after Slaughter-month, in which the superfluous cattle had been killed and their meat stored for future use. So far as can be guessed from later usages, the only ones of which we have direct knowledge, it was a time of feasting and of rites intended to counteract the darkness and cold of winter and assist the coming of brighter weather. This is characteristic rather of Northern than of Southern Europe, for obvious climatic reasons. The prominence even now of lights and green decorations at Christmas seem to be survivals of this ancient native magic.

Roman and Christian influence now provided the northern people with a calendar date around which such usages might centre. The Mithraic festival of December 25th, the Birthday of the Invincible Sun (see p. 139), had been politicly taken over by Christianity, with a characteristic piece of re-interpretation. The Sun in question was in future not to be the Persian god, but the Sun of Righteousness spoken of by the prophet Malachi, which by the quaint methods of interpretation then and for long after in use was identified with Christ. There being no plain indication in the Gospels of the time of year when the Nativity took place, there was nothing to prevent its being fixed on that date, and this was accordingly done, and some ingenious if unsound chronological arguments found to support it. To a festival thus Christianised there could be no ecclesiastical objection, such as continued to attach to New Year's Day, at all events in those regions where beast-masquerades were prominent and popular. Hence to keep Christmas, or rather the Christmas season, the Twelve Days from then to Epiphany (January 5th) was a procedure which combined pious observance with the maintenance of old local custom, and thus what had not been originally the chief Christian festival by any means (that is rather Holy Week and Easter) became the most lastingly popular in the north. The later stages of its history, for instance its attraction, under Protestant influence, to itself of the observances of St. Nicholas' Day (December 6th), the transfer to it of divinations belonging either to New Year's Day or to the older Yule season, the Presbyterian objections to it, which have had the quaint result of giving New Year's Day its old importance again, at least in Scotland, and, latest phenomenon of all, the spread of the German Christmas tree to other countries, cannot be gone into here. They are interesting, but their investigation is full of traps for the incautious, since it is but too easy, if several customs closely resemble each other, to suppose them historically connected when no descent can be proved for the later ones from the older. The complete history of Christmas can never be written, because so much that is probably contributory to its customs was never recorded and so cannot be examined by a modern researcher, dependent as he must be upon documents for events of antiquity or the early Middle Ages. I have attempted no more than a brief outline of those features in this venerable festival which seem to have a real connexion with usages belonging, if not to Rome itself, at least with some of the motley populations of the Empire.

Of influence of the earliest, or native, religion of Rome on later times there is not much. A tendency, rather than a survival, which it has in common with existing beliefs is, as has been suggested with a good deal of plausibility, the somewhat minute distribution of functions among certain popular saints. Thus, although several saints are reputed in general to heal diseases, St. Agatha is popularly invoked to cure pains in the uterus, St. Apollonia to cure toothache, St. Clare can help sore eyes, St. Eutropius dropsy, St. Helena haemorrhage, while so great a saint as Peter the apostle has

developed a speciality under one of his titles ; as St. Peter
in Vinculis he can so influence thieves as to make them
restore the stolen property. All these examples are from the
Vosges and were living beliefs in the nineteenth century, if
not later. It would be rash in the extreme to find here a
survival of actual Roman cult or theology, as instanced in
the minute division of functions between deities mentioned
in our first chapter. As there explained, that was by no means
wholly popular, but in large measure an artificial priestly
development. But such a development seems to have rested
upon a real tendency in the people, and it is not too much
to say that a like frame of mind is to be found in this and
similar phenomena of later date. What has survived here,
then, is not the ancient religion itself, but some part of the
mentality which made it acceptable.

Another survival took a form characteristic of the credulity
of both late antiquity and the Dark and Middle Ages which
succeeded it. The learned magic which was common throughout the Roman Empire was not forgotten, but continued in
quite recognisable forms, heavily frowned upon by Church
and State alike—the Church finally forged a very efficacious
weapon against it by equating it with heresy and thus beginning the organised and widespread persecution of witches
and wizards—but persisting, the more so as unbelievers in
the reality of the Black Art were scarcely to be found until
well after the Revival of Letters. Learned theory on this
point was in its essence a continuation of the Greek, or
Graeco-Oriental, system of demonology which had been
widely accepted from about the fourth century B.C. onwards
and was all but universal towards the end, being given forms
different in detail but the same in their fundamental principles
by Christians and pagans alike. A natural conclusion there-
from, since it was also an accepted doctrine that the pagan
gods were evil spirits, was the popular impression that the
learned and famous men of antiquity were all "philosophers"
and so versed in occult arts. Vergil held a high place among
these sages, according to a tradition which seems to spread
from Naples, the city where he was buried, and become
known about the middle of the twelfth century ; to take but

one small instance of his expertise, that interesting twelfth-century guide-book, the *Wonders of Rome* (*Mirabilia Romae*), informs visitors that the Viminal is the spot where

Virgilius, being taken by the Romans, went forth invisibly and departed to Naples, whence comes the saying "Go to Naples".

But all manner of other writers, including Galen, Hippokrates and many more, both Greek and Roman, had a like reputation. One bit of magic connected with Vergil had a long life. Any book which is reputed to contain great wisdom may on occasion be used as an oracle ; the consultant opens it at random, puts his finger on a word or words and looks to see what they are, interpreting them with as much ingenuity as he requires or possesses into an answer to whatever question is troubling him. Homer was so used occasionally by Greeks, the Bible in many Christian communities. The Latin oracle was Vergil ; we have instances of his being consulted before the close of the classical period, and that practice was not extinct in the seventeenth century, though the ancient method was not, apparently, the random opening of a book but the picking up, at a shrine, of one of a number of slips or counters on each of which a Vergilian passage was written. This is but one form of divination (not counting astrology) which has come down from antiquity, as witness the following instance. In A.D. 371, the emperors Valens and Valentinian, badly frightened by information of a conspiracy against them, made vigorous enquiries, assisted by the utmost cruelty towards the accused. One piece of evidence which the judges were offered was this. Two of the culprits, Patricius and Hilarius, after performing certain elaborate rites, had placed on a table a metal dish having the letters of the Greek alphabet around its edge. Over this a diviner held a ring hung on a linen thread, and the consultants noted towards which letters it swung. The consultation was highly successful, for it spelled out answers to their questions in Greek hexameters. Thus encouraged, they boldly asked who the next Emperor was to be, and the ring obligingly spelled out TH-E-O-D, which satisfied them, for they made sure it was Theodorus, one of the Imperial secretaries. Doubtless the apparatus, if allowed to go on, would have undeceived them and explained that it meant Theodosius, who actually became Emperor in 379 along with Gratian and sole Emperor not many years later. But the interesting feature for us is that the device is one of the many varieties of what is now called a ouija-board. A simpler form of it is still used, not for grave matters of State, but for the more modest end of discovering whether a given egg will hatch a male or a female chicken. It is one of several modes of divination which depend on the accidental movements of some object suspended from a string or laid on a smooth surface where a slight force will push it one way or another; the planchette is an allied method.

Still commoner, perhaps, are the charms which are still to be found up and down Europe and once were widely and firmly believed in. All their most characteristic features— words of power which are partly foreign names (Biblical and other), partly gibberish, narratives of the doings of some holy or powerful person, with an application to the needs of the operator ("as such-a-one mastered this disease, so may it be cured in the present case") and so forth are to be paralleled in antiquity. Besides these verbal spells, some of the best-known features of witchcraft descend from antiquity, for instance *envoûtement*, or harming a person by making a wax or other figure to represent him and injuring it. The powers attributed to witches and other uncanny beings are much the same whether we get examples from ancient superstitions or mediaeval and post-mediaeval treatises on the subject. For example, their reputed power of turning themselves or someone else into the likeness of a beast is attested by several ancient stories, and was so widely believed still when Reginald Scot printed his *Discoverie of Witchcraft* in 1584 that, as he says,

these examples and reasons might put us in doubt, that everie asse, woolfe, or cat that we see, were a man, a woman, or a child.

For which reason he spends not a little space in heaping up arguments from the theology and science of his day to show such changes to be impossible.

But such survivals as these are really of little significance. They are not specifically Roman beliefs and practices which passed to a later age, hardly even Graeco-Roman, for they contained many foreign elements in antiquity. It is more to the point to ask if in the religion of Western Europe there can be detected any features which can reasonably be traced to Rome, other than the circumstance that the most numerous Christian communion has its headquarters at the Vatican and uses Latin as its official language. I think such characteristics can be detected. The main stream of Western Christianity, Catholicism in its wider sense, seems to me to have not a few inheritances from the spirit of ancient Rome and its most normal ways of thought and action. To begin with, it is a disciplined body, holding fast to certain doctrines and rites which it regards as fundamental and indispensable and claims to have inherited from the earliest times. It is therefore legalistic and conservative, characteristics which have more than once made for obscurantism and resistance to natural and inevitable change, but have on the whole contributed to its great stability and its power to outlive one rival after another. Its conservatism has not prevented development, for new doctrines have from time to time been approved, although the theory is always that they were implicit from the beginning and the innovation is simply their explicit statement. Ritual has shown, always within certain bounds, a like elasticity. All this might, with very little change, be asserted of Roman law and custom, both sacral and secular, for novelty in both those fields was apt to take the outward form of mere interpretation. Another shape which its legalism has taken is insistence on proper established form ; in the administration, especially, of its sacraments it prescribes, and from very early times has prescribed, a right and approved way of doing and saying what is necessary, and denies validity to any different method, save within very clearly fixed limits. There is always a written text to appeal to, and that text is guaranteed by the express approval of competent authority. The College of Pontiffs, could it be brought back to see its successors, would heartily agree, for it also had its texts, whereof not one syllable might be altered without vitiating the whole rite ; the very term "vitiate" is adapted from the technical Latin word *uitium*, signifying a flaw.

But there is perhaps even more in it than that. Beyond all the definiteness of dogmas and creeds and the exactitude of rituals and prayers, the ceremonies of historical Christianity leave room for a mind perceptive to such influences to feel the presence or influence of something not to be caught in meshes of words or more than hinted at in actions. Here, then, after the centuries of development, we are in a sense back where we started ; the pious worshipper at a Pontifical Mass may still feel, with the Roman farmer of pre-Republican days, that *numen* is present.

FINIS

LITERATURE

(A) General Accounts

English is well supplied with these. They include: F. ALTHEIM, *A History of Roman Religion*, translated H. Mattingly (original, often very unorthodox, in its views), 1938; C. BAILEY, *Phases in the Religion of ancient Rome*, 1932; CARTER, JESSE BENEDICT, *The Religion of Numa, and other Essays on the Religion of ancient Rome*, 1906; FOWLER, W. WARDE, *Roman Festivals of the period of the Republic* (standard English work, now slightly out of date), ed. 2, 1908; HALLIDAY, WILLIAM REGINALD, *Lectures on the history of Roman Religion*, 1922.

(B) Interpretative

BAILEY, *Religion in Virgil*, 1935; CARTER, *The religious life of Ancient Rome*, 1912; FOWLER, *The Religious experience of the Roman People*, 1911; *Roman ideas of Deity*, 1914; WAGENVOORT, H., *Roman Dynamism* (treats the idea of *numen* especially), 1947 (for this book the Dutch edition, *Imperium*, 1941, was used).

(C) Particular Points

Oriental and mystery-cults; CUMONT, F., *After Life in Roman Paganism*, 1928; *Les religions orientales dans le paganisme romain*, ed. 4, 1929 (excellently annotated; the English translation by Grant Showerman, 1911, is from an earlier and less well documented edition). Calendar festivals; FRAZER, SIR J. G., *The Fasti of Ovid*, 5 vols., 1929; numerous points are discussed, with ethnological parallels, in his other works, notably *The Golden Bough*, ed. 3, 13 vols., 1911-1936. Miscellaneous problems; ROSE, H. J., *The Roman Questions of Plutarch*, 1924. Survivals of savage customs in classical times; same, *Primitive Culture in Italy*, 1926. Survivals of Roman customs, etc., into post-classical times; HALLIDAY, *Greek and Roman Folklore*, 1927; SPARGO, JOHN WEBSTER, *Virgil the Necromancer*, 1934. On the history of Christmas there is no good work in English.

INDEX

(References in bold face type are of importance.)

ABRAHAM, 144
abstraction(s), 9, 101 (ff)
Academics, 103
Actium, 112, 134
Aemilia (Vestal), 23
Aeneas, Aineias, 55, 94
Aesculapius, Asklepios, 97
Agatha, St., 152
agonium, 64
Agrippina, 121
Ahriman, 139
Ahura Mazda, 140
Aias, 10
Aius Locutius, 24
Alba Longa, 88
Alexander the Great, 101, 137
Alexander Severus, Emperor, 144
Alexandria, Alexandrians, 134, 136
Alps, 65
altar, 20 (f), 36
Ambarvalia, 35(f), 57, 62, 64, 145
Amburbium, 57
animism, 12
Anio (Aniene), river, 126
Anna Perenna, 83
Anna, sister of Dido, 83
Antium (Anzio), 53, 91
Antoninus, M. Aurelius, Emperor, 119
Antony, Mark (M. Antonius), 105, 111, 134
ancilia, 66
Anubis, 134
Aphrodite, 74, 93 (f), 98, 133 ; Antheia, 74
Apollo, 94 (ff), 98, 107, 112, 125, 146
Apollonia, St., 152
Apuleius, L., 133, 134 (f)
Aquarius, 115
Arcadius, Emperor, 148
Ares, 62, 67, 98
Argei, 80
Aricia, 90
Aristophanes, 141
Arkadians, 15
Armenia, 118
Armilustrium, 66
Artemis, 90, 98, 110
Arval Brothers (*Fratres aruales*), 86 (f)

Arx, 71
Aryans, 24
astrology, 112, 113 (ff), 140, 149
Athena, 55, 59, 98, 133
Athens, Athenians, 26, 32, 133
Attalos, 125
Atticus, T. Pomponius, 102
Attis, 125 (ff)
Audrey, John, 145
Augurs, 65 (f), 105
Augustus, Emperor, 13, 15, 67, 86, 95, 98, 103 (f), 106 (ff), 134, 143
Ausonius, D. Magnus, 146
auspicium, 86
Automatia, 101
Aventine (*Mons Auentinus*), 15, 63, 71, 74, 84, 90

BACCHUS, Bakchos, 37, 72, 130 : see Dionysos, Liber Pater
Bailey, Dr. C., 109
Bartolemeo, S., 97
Basil, St., 150
Benedict, St., 146
Bible, references to, 141, 142, 151, 154, 155
birth, ceremonial of, 41 (f)
bronze, Bronze Age, 60, 89
Brutus, L. Junius, 105
bulla, 39

CACA, Cacus, 80
Caecidius, M., 23
Caelian (*Mons Caelius*), 63, 84
calendar, 51 (ff), 147, 150
Caligula (Gaius), Emperor, 134
Camillus, M. Furius, 84, 102
Campus Martius, 63, 98, 134
Candelifera, 41
Capitol (*Mons Capitolinus*), 15, 17, 18, 21, 27, 49 (f), 59, 71, 90, 95, 102
Cappadocia, 128
Capricorn, 114
Carmentis, 31
Castor and Pollux, 91
Cassino, Monte, 146
Cato, M. Porcius, censor, 62, 89
Catullus, C. Valerius, 32
Ceres, 14, 25, 26, 37, 71 (ff), 96, 99